LITTLE ELSE
THAN A MEMORY

LITTLE ELSE THAN A MEMORY

Purdue Students Search for the Class of 1904

EDITED BY KRISTINA BROSS

TWO THOUSAND
AND FOURTEEN

THE HONORS COLLEGE
PURDUE UNIVERSITY
WEST LAFAYETTE, INDIANA

> This book is typeset in Caslon and Centaur, fonts favored by Bruce Rogers. The American typographer received a BS from Purdue University in 1890. He created Centaur around 1914.

Copyright 2014 by Purdue University. All rights reserved.
Printed in the United States of America.

Cataloging-in-Publication Data is on file at the Library of Congress.
　　Print ISBN: 978-1-62671-014-6
　　ePUB ISBN: 978-1-62671-012-2
　　ePDF ISBN: 978-1-62671-013-9

Cover design by Kelsey Schnieders.

Production Editors:
　　Tim Bolton
　　Brooke Halteman
　　Abigael Johnson
　　Kasey Kaisershot
　　Paige Pope
　　Kelsey Schnieders

The production editors were all students in the Honors College publishing course, spring 2014.

Contents

Preface ... vii

Introduction ... 1

A Tale of Two Satterfields:
The Power of a Purdue Education ... 37
Eden Holmes

"The Only Colored Drug Store":
Richard Wirt Smith's Success Story, 1904–1911 ... 55
Maggie Mace

Emil Farkas and William Raymond Davis:
Windy City Boys ... 73
Emily Durkin

Joseph Burke Knapp:
"A Barnacle on the Ship of Progress" ... 89
Alexandria Nickolas

Fitting In but Sticking Out: The Life of an
Immigrant Student at Purdue in 1904   105
   Lindy Schubring

Far from Home and Far from Normal:
The Experience of an International Student
on an American College Campus at the Turn
of the Twentieth Century   121
   Vivian Gu

Lyla Vivian Marshall Harcoff:
The Pursuits of a Small-Town Dreamer   135
   Carolyn Griffith

"The Eternal Feminine": An Examination of the
Life and Tmes of the Twentieth-Century New
University Woman through Cecil Clare Crane   155
   Cedar Marie Woodworth

The Lost Bandsman and His Band   181
   Paige Zimmerman

Just Harry   195
   Lily Anderson

Epilogue: Purdue's Past through
Purdue's Present   213
   Susan Curtis

Biographical Cameos   223

Preface

THIS BOOK REFLECTS a unique classroom collaboration. In fall 2013 I was asked to teach the inaugural offering of "Interdisciplinary Approaches to Writing" for Purdue's new Honors College. As I thought about the many learning outcomes for the class (analytical and argumentative writing skills, information literacy), it seemed to be especially important to immerse the students in original research and to encourage them to make original arguments. I have found no better way of engaging students in the acts of research and writing than by equipping them to make discoveries for themselves rather than asking them only to reconstruct or refine those of others. But it is a challenge to find a way for undergraduates in an introductory class to perform independent research, especially in my fields of literary studies and American studies. Unlike my colleagues in science or technology, I do not have a lab in which students can apprentice by taking charge of a part of a larger research question I have already identified. Archival research is ideal for the goal of original work, especially in local archives, since such collections often go unexamined by scholars interested in broader contexts or better known historical figures.

And so I turned to the Purdue University Virginia Kelly Karnes Archives and Special Collections as the ground of our work together in the class. As we talked about the structure of introductions or the best ways to cite sources, the students also completed exercises such as a library "scavenger hunt" in which they tracked down obscure sources of information in the periodical stacks, online databases, special collections, or book holdings. For the midterm assignment, I constructed an "object analysis" in which students spent time with scrapbooks produced by Purdue students from the turn of the twentieth century, chose a postcard, photo, advertisement, or other "scrap," researched it, and wrote a mock grant proposal based on their early research results.

After such preliminaries, we turned the rest of the semester over to the main project of the course: to select, research, and critically examine the life story of a member of Purdue's class of 1904. To do so, students

Figure 1. Students from the class examine hundred-year-old scrapbooks from the Purdue Libraries Archives and Special Collections.

had to immerse themselves in the the Purdue Libraries Archives and Special Collections. They consulted genealogy sources, wrote to descendants, and combed scholarly databases for contextual studies to help make sense of the details of the lives they uncovered. Most importantly, they had to answer the ever difficult "so what" question: for readers who are not descendants of the subject or who may not care about Purdue, why is the life story of Lyla Vivian Marshall Harcoff, Hugo Berthold, or Frederic Henry Miller significant?

Ten of the resulting essays have been collected for this book. The research and writing process was by turns exciting and frustrating, and the students' responses to the question of significance are, I believe, good ones. Yet few if any of the authors consider their research complete. Most of the students were in their first years (and first semesters) at Purdue when they took the class. Most have suggested to me since that they hope to return to the project and expand on these findings, either through independent study, in intermediate undergraduate research supported by one of Purdue's grant programs, or as part of their senior theses. In short, I am sure that as we follow up on this initial research, we will uncover more information, discover mistakes, and revise our initial understanding of the experiences of the class of 1904.

When the class began, we had no intention of publishing these pieces. My syllabus indicated that we would present our research to a wider public in some way, but we were imagining a small exhibition or a series of talks. However, about midway through the term Charles Watkinson, head of Purdue Libraries' Scholarly Publishing Services, and Catherine Fraser Riehle, associate professor of library science, contacted me about their Honors College class, a "Publishing Bootcamp." Their class is designed to introduce Purdue undergraduates to the scholarly publishing industry, not only to open new career options, but also to help them develop as the academic authors of the future. A significant feature of the course is to give students the hands-on experience of editing and producing a book. As we talked, we realized that a partnership between the two classes would be an excellent fit and would support Purdue's larger goals of supporting undergraduate research across the University. My class has been especially enthusiastic about sharing these early results of their findings with a wider readership. Moreover, although I am not an instructor for the publishing class, it seems clear that the students in that course have gained much from their firsthand experience about the joys and frustrations of taking written drafts to polished completion. All in all, I can say that this classroom experiment has been a wonderful experience, one that we hope to reprise in the future.

Classroom innovations such as this one are rarely solo endeavors. I owe thanks to many at Purdue for helping to make it possible. Thanks go especially to the Honors College for initiating and supporting both courses, and to the English Department for releasing me from me from one of my regular courses. Collaborating with Charles Watkinson and Catherine Fraser Riehle, the instructors of record for the publishing course, as well as with Katherine Purple, Purdue University Press's managing editor, has been a delight. Thanks also to Kelley Kimm, production editor; Jennifer Lynch, editorial assistant; and Teresa Brown, photographer in the Libraries.

The student members of the publishing class have been professional, enthusiastic, and unbelievably fast as they worked on drafts and proofs. Neither the class nor the book would have been possible without the support of Purdue Libraries Archives and Special Collections. My thanks to Sammie Morris, associate professor and University archivist, and her staff as a whole for allowing us space, access, and research assistance. My deep appreciation goes to digital archivist Neal Harmeyer, who seemed to wave a magic wand and create electronic copies of key archival sources, and who mentored the student researchers, especially in the final crucial weeks of the course. As the students thought about the genre of biography and considered how they could best represent their subjects, they benefited greatly from a panel of experts who shared their experiences in life writing. Our thanks to Professor Thomas Broden, Professor Susan Curtis, and especially to Purdue alumni Elizabeth Hudson (class of 2012) and Angie Klink (class of 1981). These alumni authors were especially important models for our class. Both have published their research out of Purdue's archives and offered firsthand knowledge of the riches of Purdue's history and special collections as well as the challenges of wrestling it into shape for readers.

Two individuals merit special thanks. Archivist Elizabeth Wilkinson was my team-teacher in all but name, collaborating with me on the construction of the syllabus, attending every class to offer her expertise, and offering advice and support to the students as they tackled this ambitious project. Her enthusiasm and excitement for our research experiment helped them—and me—get over the rough spots. Finally, I want to offer my gratitude once again to my colleague and friend Susan Curtis. We began thinking about ways to use local archives and special collections in our classes over a decade ago, and we have since team-taught several graduate seminars using West Lafayette and Purdue materials. My philosophy and approach to this class have been shaped by that partnership. When we considered the contents for this volume, I knew that it would be best completed with her reflection on our work. I am grateful for her deep knowledge, rigor, and especially for the generosity she brings to us as a historian of the period our subjects knew as the "naughty naughts."

KRISTINA BROSS
Associate Professor
College of Liberal Arts
Purdue University

Introduction

The book you hold in your hands is a supercharged family history, a time-traveling scrapbook, a report from a temporary laboratory of life writing tucked away on the fourth floor of the Humanities, Social Sciences, and Education (HSSE) Library in Purdue University's Stewart Center. Each of the genres—family history, scrapbook, lab report—offers a different lens on Purdue's past, and each provides different answer to the question of what that past means to us today.

The Super-Charged Family History

We tell and trace family histories because we believe that our ancestors have in some way shaped who we are today. We record family histories as a way of paying respect to (or perhaps seeking justice for) those who have gone before us. And in some ways we care about our family histories, because in doing so we make a claim on the future for ourselves: because we remember the past, we hope that those to come will remember us. We look at pictures of our great-great-grandparents and see the shape of our own noses or chins. We hear stories of sibling rivalries, businesses begun (or failed), character traits, or traditions of family names, and we gain a glimpse of the forces that have shaped us. As we researched the lives of students in Purdue's past, we couldn't help but compare the experiences of today to those of 1904, and we couldn't help but imagine some future in which other undergraduate researchers would sift through the trace remains of our lives to better understand 2014. (And since we weren't visited by a time-traveling research team, we must assume that those researchers of the future will still be doing things old school.)

During the school year of 1903–1904, the University enrolled about 1,400 students. The class of 1904 numbered about 230.[1] They hailed from Indiana, of course, but also from Ohio, Illinois, Kentucky, Wash-

Figure 1. An overview of campus buildings from the early 1900s. Courtesy of Purdue Libraries Archives and Special Collections.

ington, Texas, and beyond. At least three students were what we'd classify today as "international" students, from Bulgaria, the United Kingdom, and Japan. Others were identified as immigrants or children of immigrants. Two students were African American men, and eight women were pictured in the senior section of the 1904 Purdue student yearbook, the *Debris*—"coeds" in the parlance of the day.

The rhythm of life at the University included classes, of course. But then as now, extracurricular forces made as much of an impression. For male students, campus routine included military drilling in "The Corp." For the women students, it included supervision and restrictions on gentleman callers in the Ladies' Hall residence.[2] White men had the option of living on or near campus in the dorm or fraternity houses. For the few African American students enrolled at Purdue during these years, their pursuit of education would have included a commute—neither Purdue nor West Lafayette would house students of color until decades later.[3] Until the opening of the Eliza Fowler assembly hall, students and faculty convened for daily fifteen-minute chapel meetings.[4] Fowler Hall enabled Purdue to establish weekly one-hour convocations, which were, as Purdue's student newspaper noted, "a feature of the larger universities of the East that has much to do with the interest that so distinguishes them from some of the younger western institutions." That same article goes on to support President Stone's ban on "class yells" at the convocations, urging students to give over some of their class rivalry for whole-school spirit: "We will have class antagonism and lots of it, but let every Purdue man help develop a Purdue unity of spirit. . . . Let's have Bully for Old Purdue loud and long."[5]

Class identity was as important, if not more so, than a general Boilermaker identity, as evidenced by the threat of class yells in so dignified a setting as the Eliza Fowler auditorium and by the need to remind students to call for "Old Purdue loud and long." Varsity teams were avidly supported, but each class made up its own baseball, track, and other sports teams for intramural play. Class pride, male physical prowess, and militancy combined as an institution in the annual "Tank Scrap," a campus ritual that opened Purdue's unofficial school year calendar from 1894–1914.[6] During the Tank Scrap, sophomore men squared off against freshmen in a fight—a physical fight—to win the right to paint the class year in huge letters on the municipal water tank about a mile from campus.

FIGURE 2. TANK SCRAP. COURTESY OF PURDUE LIBRARIES ARCHIVES AND SPECIAL COLLECTIONS.

If in 1904 the Tank Scrap launched the school year, the Mechanics Burning brought it to a close. This particular rite of passage brought together the senior engineers, all of whom took mechanics and hydraulics as part of their required curriculum. In order to celebrate the end of the course and their impending graduation, they burned their textbooks and the authors in effigy, accompanying the conflagration with a spoof of a funeral ceremony, complete with parodied funeral orations.[7]

Between the Tank Scrap and the Mechanics Burning, there were trips to Chicago, dances arranged by classes and organizations, YMCA meetings, and a series of special events held at Fowler Hall, a forerunner of today's Convocations series of performances.[8] One of the most eagerly anticipated and elaborate entertainment was the Purdue minstrel show—a student talent show that included performances by the mandolin club as well as skits parodying race and ethnicity, characteristic of such performances nationwide. One is left

FIGURE 3. THE FIRST MECHANICS BURNING. COURTESY OF PURDUE LIBRARIES ARCHIVES AND SPECIAL COLLECTIONS.

to speculate on the effect such a show might have had on the students of color, especially African American students already contending with segregated housing and other forms of discrimination.

Seniors worked on their theses. Everyone graduated with a BS degree, but it's clear from the range of projects, which included an essay on the "Idealism of George Sand" as well as a proposal for "A Tunnel Under the Chicago River" and an "Investigation of the Coefficient of Expansion in Concrete," that not everyone wanted to pursue what we'd call the STEM— science, technology, engineering, and math—disciplines today. The goal of a land-grant university, after all, was to give its students a full university education, and even students dedicated to creating a plan for "An Interurban Railway Project from Lafayette Indiana to Hoopeston, Illinois" perceived gaps in the technological education they were offered. They filled in their education with memberships in the various literary societies—the Emerson, Irving, and Philalethean— highly visible social groups that organized talks and concerts and gave students practice in writing essays on cultural and philosophical topics.

However important the cultivation of the mind, college life in the early twentieth century placed equal emphasis on physical development. As historian John

Kasson argues, interest in sports among men exploded during this period. Sports were considered a lynchpin of masculine identity: "In boisterous play and aggressive competitions, bachelors could enjoy a continuity between boyhood and manhood. They played or watched sports and reveled in contests of physical skill and decisive triumph."[9] Then as now, Purdue's varsity sports teams were the source of entertainment and the object of boosterism.

This list of activities and interests at Purdue in 1903–1904 suggests the privilege that the students enjoyed. During their undergrad years, students were exempt from many of the responsibilities and cares of their working peers. But no matter how absorbing the studies and clubs were, college life is never just an ivory-tower existence, a point brought home to the mem-

FIGURE 4. STUDIO PORTRAIT OF "LONG JOHN" MILLER AND HARRY LESLIE, KEY MEMBERS OF THE VARSITY FOOTBALL TEAM. FROM JOHN MILLER'S SCRAPBOOK, COURTESY OF PURDUE LIBRARIES ARCHIVES AND SPECIAL COLLECTIONS.

bers of the class of 1904 by a tragedy early in the year. On October 31, Purdue was scheduled to play its long-term rival Indiana University in a football game in Indianapolis. A special train chartered to bring the team, the band, and nearly a thousand fans to the game was wrecked when it hit a much heavier coal train head on, splintering the first car, which carried the team, and resulting in the death of seventeen and injuries to many more.

Figure 5. Purdue train wreck image. Courtesy of Purdue Libraries Archives and Special Collections.

Physical recovery took a long time. Harry Leslie, the strapping young football player who posed with his friend John Miller a year or so earlier (see figure 4), was one of the most severely wounded. He went on to become governor of Indiana, but he never lost the limp caused by his injuries in 1903. And we can only imagine the emotional effects such a tragedy took on a much smaller and close-knit Purdue community. Indeed, the Purdue special collections has an unused ticket from that game, donated in the 1960s by alumnus Frank W. Willey. In the letter that accompanied the donation, he writes that "No Halloween in the past 60 years has passed without a quiet thought in memory of Purdue in 1903."[10]

If the year began in tragedy, it ended with optimism about Purdue's role on a national and even international stage. In the spring, students and faculty from across the campus were busy with preparations for Purdue's showing at the 1904 World's Fair in St. Louis, which opened on April 30—the *Debris* of 1905 reported proudly of Purdue's success at the fair. The *Debris* also reported on the visit of Prince Pu Lun, heir to the Chinese throne, who made a stop at Purdue en route to the fair.[11]

Read Purdue's *Debris* yearbook from 1904 and 1905. And read—as the authors of the essays in this book did—all the issues of the 1903–1904 student newspaper, the *Exponent*. Track down pictures, dance cards, and senior theses, and the story that emerges of

Purdue's class of 1904 will seem much like any family history, registering by turns milestones and losses, including the best of what family can offer—connection, support, love—and also less happy reflections of the times—violence, racism, sexism, xenophobia. The editors of the 1904 *Debris* wrote in their "Greeting" that they saw themselves as documenting "that happiest phase of existence—the life of the college undergraduate," and that they wrote as "members of that body which is so soon to become little else than a memory—the class of 1904."[12] As the recipients of this family history, we have tried to resurrect that memory, and we acknowledge the connections of our own moment to that of our institutional great-great-great-grandparents—the good, the bad, and the in-between.

FIGURE 6. PRINCE PU LUN (*DEBRIS* 1905, 22). COURTESY OF PURDUE LIBRARIES ARCHIVES AND SPECIAL COLLECTIONS.

Time-Traveling Scrapbook

If a family history pieces together information from the past to tell us a story about our roots, a scrapbook offers something else. A scrapbook seems a more concrete link to the past. John Miller, class of 1903, actually clipped articles, collected souvenirs, took a glue pot, and pasted these items into his book. When we page through his scrapbook, we feel some sort of connection. We feel that we are getting a behind-the-scenes, personal glimpse of his reality so long ago.

At the same time, a century-old scrapbook is profoundly *un*satisfying. We can speculate about why John Miller collected sports clippings featuring his successes, but what on earth does a hand-painted jack-o-lantern have to do with anything (see figure 7)? Scrapbooks in all their personal, gnomic glory are frustrating for researchers. They tantalize, but they often seem to be missing just the piece of information that we need to make sense of the past as collected in the pages.

Historians sometimes talk about archives as gold mines—they go seeking "treasures" from the past—or as an uncharted country ripe for "discoveries." Indeed, I used that exact metaphor in the preface to describe how I hoped the students in this class would feel about their work. But these metaphors, which suggest that the rewards for historical research are in proportion to our

FIGURE 7. PAGE FROM JOHN MILLER'S SCRAPBOOK. COURTESY OF PURDUE LIBRARIES ARCHIVES AND SPECIAL COLLECTIONS.

efforts, simply don't work. Our experiences when writing this book suggest that the idea of the scrapbook is a better image; what traces of the past we encounter in the archives survive as much because of idiosyncratic choice or happenstance or even for political reasons as they do because of conscious attempts to remember and preserve the past. The collections of a scrapbook exist because someone got a Brownie camera and decided to snap and keep photos of an outing to Happy Hollow Park, or because someone rushed the Phi Delta Theta fraternity, and because he was in his late teens and early twenties, fraternity hijinks and dance cards seemed especially important events to remember.[13] Or the past may survive in special collections and become available to researchers only because of an amazing sequence of events. During the course of her research, Alexandria Nickolas found the e-mail address of her subject's grandson. They had several conversations, and the next thing we knew, Alex was opening a package mailed to her that contained Joseph Knapp's 1903 scrapbook. For the rest of the semester it was on loan to Purdue Libraries, and it is now in the process of being permanently donated. Certainly the family had kept and treasured the book, but if not for the class assignment, if not for Alexandria's choice of Joseph Knapp from among more than two hundred other possible subjects, if not for the particular path of research she chose, we likely would not have this rich resource available to a wider readership.

On the flip side: traces of the past may not exist to be uncovered. We may not even know what we are missing. Scrapbooks are always incomplete in that they reflect a particular, personal point of view of what's valuable, and few collectors think to treasure the everyday objects that can give us a sense of how people lived in the past. Even when collectors and archivists have been diligent, even if we have all the space in the world to hold and protect the papers, photographs, and ephemera that help us reconstruct the past, time will take its toll. In the scrapbook, glue loosens, fasteners give way, paper tears, items slip out. Still, all is not lost. Carolyn Steedman, author of *Dust: The Archive and Cultural History*, reminds us that even absence in an archive carries meaning. She argues "that if we find nothing [in the archives] we will find nothing in a place; and then, that an absence is not *nothing*, but is rather the space left by what has gone: how the emptiness indicates how once it was filled and animated."[14] The scrapbook metaphor is useful once again to help make sense of this seeming paradox. We might think of a page from which a newspaper clipping, photo, or other object has been lost, but on which we can still see its faded outline, the space left by what has gone.[15]

Up until now, I've been speaking of historical information that we know existed but that we can no longer access. Over the course of the semester, we also grappled with aspects of our subjects' lives that had never been documented. In these cases, Steedman's argument that we consider the "space left by what has gone" was even more important—and even more difficult. Consider the biography of Clifford Harry Evans (below), another member of the class of 1904, and one of the two African American men to graduate that year.

His *Debris* biography, unlike those of most other students, reveals almost nothing about his time at Purdue. But if we turn our attention away from what exists in the Purdue Libraries Archives and Special Collections about this student, and consider instead

CLIFFORD HARRY EVANS, B. S. in Mechanical Engineering.
Thesis: Various Temperatures of Water in Locomotive Boilers.
Evans comes from Terre Haute. He is a Republican and a Methodist, but answers "yes" to nearly all the vices on the catalogue. Throughout his four years at Purdue he has pursued a consistent policy of attending to his own business to the exclusion of all other affairs, in which respect he has furnished an example by which many of the rest of us could profit. He will be a teacher.

FIGURE 8. A PAGE FROM JOHN MILLER'S SCRAPBOOK WITH THE OUTLINE OF A LOST OBJECT (BOTTOM LEFT). COURTESY OF PURDUE LIBRARIES ARCHIVES AND SPECIAL COLLECTIONS.

the "nothing in a place" that characterizes Evans' archival record at Purdue, we may be able to understand more about his life, or at least to speculate about it. The fact that he is not listed as participating in any clubs or campus activities may be significant. His determination to "keep to himself" is certainly unusual among students in the class of 1904. As Lindy Schubring argues in her study of Hugo Berthold, even students singled out (and perhaps mocked) for their immigrant status or ethnicity participated in extracurricular activities. What does it mean that Evans did not? What does it mean that the editors of the *Debris* felt that his allegiance to Methodism and Republicanism best characterized him? In advance of more research—research that may uncover concrete information or result in a dead end, of course—we can speculate that Evans brought his dedication to his faith and to the Republican party with him to Purdue from his hometown Terre Haute. At the turn of the century, both Terre Haute and Lafayette boasted African Methodist Churches, likely candidates for Evans' membership. And of course during the Reconstruction Era and the early twentieth century, African Americans allied themselves almost exclusively with the Republican party.[16] From these spare details we can say *something* about Evans' experiences while he was a student at Purdue, but it all has to do with his life off campus rather than on. We should also remember that Evans was not allowed to live on campus during this time—living quarters both at Purdue and in West Lafayette were segregated. It seems telling that his fellow students saw him mostly as a student who kept himself—was kept—apart from the mainstream of undergraduate life. If we have found little or nothing about Clifford Harry Evans at Purdue, we have found nothing in a place that only grudgingly admitted young men of color and—as some of the essays below will discuss—at times outright abused them.

I hope this brief digression into Clifford Harry Evans' life usefully illustrates our methodology. As a time-traveling scrapbook, this volume pieces together the traces of the past that we have been able to find on our subjects, along with speculation about what doesn't seem to have been collected or preserved in the documentary archive. We have organized the essays accordingly, not necessarily by their affinity one to another, but by a kind of scrapbooking rhythm. We have alternated subjects for whom we've located a rich archival trail and those for whom the "nothing" of the record has been as eloquent as the records, pictures, and memories of their fellow students who have left a more tangible impression on the archive.

Report from the Lab of Life Writing

Part family history, part scrapbook, this volume is even more a lab report—a report of the findings of students working in a unique liberal arts-archival laboratory. The authors of these essays may have chosen their biographical subjects for a variety of personal reasons (because they shared a hometown; because they sensed a similar unconventional approach to life; simply because they both played in the band), but as we dug into the research, that primary connection expanded, and the original connecting thread became a thick web of understanding, encompassing not only the personal details of these long-ago students, but also the historical events, popular culture, and philosophical beliefs that gave shape to their lives, and that make this collection valuable beyond the natural curiosity today's Boilermakers feel about Purdue students of yesterday.

Those of us who remember taking science classes in high school or college will remember the form of the lab report (not to mention those of us who continue to research and publish out of science and technology labs today). We are perhaps less used to thinking about the essays generated by humanities and social sciences students as similar reports of research. Yet critical thinking in these fields requires the same moves: hypothesis, data collection, analysis. Perhaps one key difference in method is that the act of research and the act of writing are not always separate processes in the humanities or social sciences, but rather, the essay is our key experimental apparatus.

So, what would the findings of this research look like laid out as a conventional lab report? Read on.

Abstract

By using the approaches and methods of critical life writing, the essays in this collection uncover a diversity of experiences among the members of Purdue's class of 1904. The research presented here suggests how the events and lives of a relatively small, midwestern, land-grant university both reflected and influenced national and even international contexts at the turn of the twentieth century.

Introduction

Few studies of land-grant universities focus on the lives and experiences of the students, unless they have distinguished themselves in extraordinary ways. At Purdue University, the lives of its famous alumni—John McCutcheon or Neil Armstrong, for instance—have been well documented, but little attention has been paid to the rank and file among its generations of students. The neglect can perhaps be attributed to a lingering sense that Ivy League or East Coast schools have been more influential in US history, or because the particular histories of land-grant institutions have seemed less important than a general accounting of the educational movement initiated by the Morrill Act. Also, until the opening of the Virginia Kelly Karnes Archives and Special Collections Research Center in 2009, it was difficult to research lesser known Purdue figures.

The essays in this book have been informed by several key theoretical approaches to archives and by critical studies of the period. I have already mentioned Steedman's book, which explores the promise and limits of the archive. Her work responds to Jacques Derrida's "Archive Fever," itself a meditation on memory, archive, and power. Although the students did not read Derrida for themselves, his ideas inform my own, and so the work was deep background for our study. In particular, we returned repeatedly to the ethical horizon of our work, to Derrida's exploration of a question first posed by Yosef Hayim Yerushalmi—"'Is it possible that the antonym of 'forgetting' is not 'remembering,' but *justice*?'"—as we pondered how best to represent and to analyze critically our subjects and their stories.[17]

Several historical studies of the early twentieth century have been helpful, but a key reading for the class as a whole was John Kasson's book *Houdini, Tarzan, and the Perfect Man*, which explores the early twentieth century's understanding of masculinity, and which links the performance of masculinity to key aspects of US modernity, such as shift in demographics from rural to urban populations, industrialization, changing gender norms, and so forth. More specifically for Purdue, we turned to Robert Topping's general history *A Century and Beyond*, though the essays presented here are both more limited in scope than his expansive work and also take an analytical rather than celebratory approach to Purdue's past. A smaller work, but one more directly applicable to our project was Ryan K. Anderson's "'The Law of College Customs is [as] Inexorable as the Laws of Chemistry or Physics': The Transition to a Modern Purdue University, 1900–1924," which we found helpful as a bridge between Kasson's more expansive treatment of culture in the United States and our own interests in a thin slice of Purdue's history.

Materials and Methods

Researchers began by selecting a short biography of a member of Purdue's class of 1904, which had been published in the school's yearbook, the *Debris* (see Appendix). These short statements gave us only the bare minimum of biographical information—full names and (usually) hometowns—along with some details of the subjects' activities while at Purdue, their majors, and the title of their senior theses, if applicable.

From these few details, our authors turned to the Purdue Libraries Archives and Special Collections. They consulted the minutes of the board of trustees, personal papers, club minutes, and the Alumni Record. They read the complete run of the 1903–04 *Exponent*, which provided many details of the culture and events of the year. They traced their subjects through genealogical resources and self-published family histories. They placed their findings in a scholarly conversation and considered several approaches to life writing.

Choosing the focus and the form of their essays was a significant part of the challenge of the research. To capture a life in five to ten pages required each author to focus on just one aspect or achievement of her subject's experiences, such as identity as immigrants or international students, careers after Purdue, or experiences as undergraduate students. As a class, we considered several models of life writing. Most were more traditional narratives—the recent biography *Steve Jobs*, the story of Mary Matthews and Lella Gaddis in the twinned biography *Divided Paths, Common Ground*. We read Saidiya Hartman's "Venus in Two Acts," which meditates on the impossibility of recovering the lives of the enslaved women of the middle passage, even as Hartman acknowledges the ethical responsibility of historical researchers to recover such lost stories. And we puzzled over Nicholas Felton's *2010 Annual Report*, a visual biography of Felton's father that employs data visualization rather than narrative text to represent and make sense of his life.[18] We found this last example particularly challenging, but intriguing and inspiring nonetheless. In fact, Kathryn Math, one of the students in the class, produced an amazing visualization of the peripatetic life of Warder Crow, a member of the class of 1904, by mining the archives and the Internet for data about his employment, marriage, service record, and the nearly dozen cross-country moves he took over the course of his life. Unfortunately, because of space and format considerations, we were not able to include her work in this volume.[19]

Results

If this section of the introduction were a real lab report, I would detail our research findings in full here. But of course, you will go on to read the essays for yourselves, so I'll offer just a brief summary. The students' essays in this volume recover the lives of individual students from the class of 1904, most of whom are remembered—if at all—by their descendants. The individual essays range in form and scope depending on the kinds of archival and other evidence that has survived. Each chapter provides factual information about its subject, but each also takes a wider view, considering the historical and cultural contexts that have helped the students to make sense of the experiences embedded in archival fragments, such as census documents, newspaper ads, Purdue student records, family histories, photographs, scrapbooks, and more. The chapters variously chronicle the experiences of exchange students, athletes, band members, and coeds. They explore the ways that Purdue students inhabited the "New Woman" identity of the turn of the century; encountered race and ethnic bias; or simply enjoyed their lives at Purdue. They variously treat their subjects as case studies of the value of an early twentieth-century land-grant education; of the rural-urban divide; and of the possibilities for upward mobility afforded midwestern students by modernity.

Rather than continuing the laboratory aspect of this work, I'd like instead to say a final word about the genre of biography, which is perhaps more in keeping with my training as a literary historian and critic. Throughout this introduction, I have used the phrase "life writing" to characterize our work. The term "biography" is likely a more familiar term, and "life writing" may just seem unnecessary jargon, but I think the specific terms may be helpful. I take the idea of "life writing" to encompass the category of biography, but also to extend to all manner of other ways of treating the experiences of historic individuals. During the semester, in the throes of difficult archival research, we didn't worry too much about the nuances of terms such as life writing, biography, or—to add one more to the mix—"microhistory," but they do have different implications. Consider the definitions offered by historian Jill Lepore: "If biography is largely founded on a belief in the singularity and significance of an individual's life and his contribution to history, microhistory is founded upon almost the opposite assumption: however singular a person's life may be, the value of examining it lies not in its uniqueness, but in its exemplariness, in how that individual's life serves as an allegory for broader issues affecting the culture as a whole."[20]

Because the students engaged in original research of relatively obscure individuals, and because I didn't know in advance how much information they would be able to find, I framed their assignment more or less as a microhistory. I assumed that even if they couldn't locate specific details about their subjects, they would be able to generalize about larger issues from even slender evidence and so produce a useful essay even from archival dead ends.

But I hadn't really counted on the emotional investment of researchers in their subjects. At the end of the semester, when I asked the students what they felt were their most important findings of the term, they duly noted the links between their subjects and greater historic movements or cultural issues of the day. But they told me that whatever they had discovered about the cultural or historical significance of their subjects' experiences, I should especially stress the great diversity among the students of 1903–1904. Now, the class of 1904 bears few of the markers of diversity that we look for today: just three international students, two African American students, and only eight women. A good handful of students came from first-generation German or Irish families. A few were first-generation themselves. Some of the students were working class, a few appear to have come from well-to-do families, but most were middling sorts in terms of family income. True, students came from states as far away as Washington and Texas, but the vast majority of the graduating class of 1904 were young, white men from Indiana of fairly modest but not impoverished means.

Nevertheless, we were struck time and time again by the varied lives and fates of our subjects. I would argue that this sense of diversity is the result of the relationship we forged with our subjects by researching and writing their lives. Simply put, you can't spend hours and hours digging through the remains of another's life without developing some kind of a relationship with that person, without that person emerging in your imagination as sharply distinct from other historical figures.

Moreover, because the students began the assignment not by locating some distant historic figure to investigate, but rather were asked to choose a former Purdue student, just like each of them, it was impossible not to treat the life story of Harry Hodges, Hugo Berthold, Sukichi Yoshisaka, or Cecil Clare Crane as anything other than "singular" and "significant." Our microhistories have thus merged with the impulses of biography to become something slightly different from either genre: the family microhistory? The microbiography?

Whatever term is best to describe these essays, one result is clear. Over the course of our semester and through the production of this book, the members of the class of 1904 have emerged from the past in all their peculiar, happy, bumpy, eccentric, lonely, ambitious, bigoted, smart, sociable selves. The class of 1904 feels diverse. Its individuals feel singular because we have come to see ourselves in them, for better or for worse. And that's as it should be. They're family, after all.

Bibliography

Anderson, Ryan K. "'The Law of College Customs is [as] Inexorable as the Laws of Chemistry or Physics': The Transition to a Modern Purdue University, 1900-1924." *Indiana Magazine of History* 99.2 (June 2003): 97–128.

Bethel AME Church, "History of Bethel AME Church in Lafayette, Indiana." Digital timeline, n.d. http://bethelamelafayette.org/.

Biographical Record and Portrait Album of Tippecanoe County, Indiana. (Chicago 1888).

"Convocation," *Exponent* (West Lafayette, IN), Sept. 16, 1903.

Derrida, Jacques, and Eric Prenowitz. "Archive Fever: A Freudian Impression." *Diacritics* 25, no. 2 (Summer 1995): 9–63.

Feltron, Nicholas. "The 2010 Annual Report." www.feltron.com/ar10_01.html.

Griner, Otis. Scrapbook. MSA 129, Otis E. Griner papers, Purdue University Libraries Archives and Special Collections.

Hartman, Saidiya. "Venus in Two Acts." *Small Axe* 12, no. 2 (June 2008): 1–14.

Heslop, Madison. "Murky Drops from Old Pump Rotten: The Old Pump, the 'Purdue Woman,' and the Ancient Order of the Dormitory Devils." *Journal of Purdue Undergraduate Research* 3 (2013). http://dx.doi.org/10.5703/jpur.03.14.07.

Hovde, David. "The Tank." Purdue University Libraries Archives and Special Collections. http://collections.lib.purdue.edu/traditions/.

Isaacson, Walter. *Steve Jobs*. New York: Simon & Schuster, 2011.

Kasson, John. *Houdini, Tarzan and the Perfect Man: The White Male Body and the Challenge of Modernity in America*. New York: Hill and Wang, 2001.

Klink, Angie. *Divided Paths, Common Ground: The Story of Mary Matthews and Lella Gaddis, Pioneering Purdue Women Who Introduced Science into the Home*. West Lafayette: Purdue University Press, 2011.

Lepore, Jill. "Historians Who Love Too Much: Reflections on Microhistory and Biography." *Journal of American History* 88, no. 1 (June 2001): 129–44.

Math, Kathryn. "As the Crow Flies: The Life of Warder Crow in Maps, Facts and Statistical Data." Unpublished essay.

McCormick, Mike. *Terre Haute, Queen of the Wabash*. Charleston: Arcadia Publishing, 2005.

Miller, Simeon. Scrapbook. MSA 21, Simeon V. B. Miller scrapbook. Purdue University Libraries Archives and Special Collections.

Steedman, Carolyn. *Dust: The Archive and Cultural History*. Manchester: Manchester University Press, 2001.

Topping, Robert W. *A Century and Beyond: The History of Purdue University*. West Lafayette: Purdue University Press, 1988.

Willey, Frank W. Letter to Purdue Librarian, October 27, 1963. Purdue University Libraries Archives and Special Collections.

Young, Lisa. "After the Debris Clears: Tracing Purdue's Early Black Student Experiences with Housing Segregation in West Lafayette." Unpublished paper.

Notes

1. I've used the number reported in the retrospective on 1903–1904 that was published in the 1905 *Debris*. This number seems likely to reflect the University's own records after the loose ends of spring graduation had been tied up. There are 218 students depicted in the senior section of the 1904 *Debris*, though several of these students are listed as being set to graduate in the next year. It's unclear to me whether those who died in the train wreck on October 31, 1903, were included in the calculations published by the editors of the 1905 *Debris*. Other sources list different totals for the senior class, but all estimate it in the range of 200 or so.

2. For more information about gender and customs at the turn of the century, see Madison Heslop, "Murky Drops from Old Pump Rotten: The Old Pump, the 'Purdue Woman,' and the Ancient Order of the Dormitory Devils," *Journal of Purdue Undergraduate Research* 3 (2013): 44–49.

3. Lisa Young's unpublished paper, "After the Debris Clears: Tracing Purdue's Early Black Student Experiences with Housing Segregation in West Lafayette," documents the segregation and desegregation of housing in West Lafayette and at Purdue. This research will be included in her PhD dissertation, presently in progress.

4. See *Debris* 1904, 17.

5. "Convocation," *Exponent* (West Lafayette, IN), Sept. 16, 1903, 9.

6. The water tank still stands today on Salisbury Street in West Lafayette. The tradition ended after the death of one of the participants. Professor David M. Hovde has conducted extensive research on Purdue's history. For more information about the Tank Scrap, see "The Tank," Purdue Libraries Archives and Special Collections, accessed March 24, 2014, http://collections.lib.purdue.edu/traditions. See also David M. Hovde, "A Manly Spectacle: Purdue University's Tank Scrap," *Traces of Indiana and Midwestern History* 26.1 (Winter 2014): 14–25.

7. For this rite and other mechanical engineering traditions, see John Norberg, ed., *Full Steam Ahead: Purdue Mechanical Engineering Yesterday, Today and Tomorrow* (West Lafayette, IN: Purdue University, 2013).

8. The first year of such events included performances and readings by musical ensembles and full orchestras, as well as readings by William Butler Yeats and James Whitcomb Riley.

9. John Kasson, *Houdini, Tarzan and the Perfect Man: The White Male Body and the Challenge of Modernity in America* (New York: Hill and Wang, 2001), 13.

10. Frank W. Willey to Purdue Librarian, October 27, 1963, MSP 117, Box 1, Folder 1, Collection of Purdue Train Wreck Materials, Purdue Libraries Archives and Special Collections.

11. See page 24 of the 1905 *Debris* for a retrospective description of Purdue's participation in the fair.

12. "Greeting," *Debris*, 1904, 5.

13. The Otis Griner scrapbook in the Purdue special collections contains several snapshots of students at Happy Hollow Park. See MSA 129, Otis E. Griner papers, Purdue Libraries Archives and Special Collections. My thanks to Maggie Mace for bringing the photos to my attention. Simeon Miller, younger brother of John Miller, pledged Phi Delt, and memorabilia from his fraternity days are included in his scrapbook. See MSA 21, Simeon V. B. Miller scrapbook, Purdue Libraries Archives and Special Collections.

14. Carolyn Steedman, *Dust: The Archive and Cultural History* (Manchester: Manchester University Press, 2001), 11.

15. After I chose this "lost" item from John Miller's scrapbook as this illustration for my point, I learned that the coin originally pasted into the book has been rescued by the Purdue Libraries Archives and Special Collections. It was found loose in the book as it was processed for digitalization, and is still a part of John Miller's papers. Thanks to Neal Harmeyer for this more up-to-date information.

16. Mike McCormick, *Terre Haute, Queen of the Wabash* (Charleston: Arcadia Publishing, 2005), 27. The African Methodist Episcopal Church in Lafayette is mentioned in the *Biographical Record and Portrait Album* (1888) as having been founded around 1849 (see page 276). On the church's historical timeline, see also the Bethel AME Church timeline, accessed March 20, 2014, http://bethelamelafayette.org/.

17. Jacques Derrida and Eric Prenowitz, "Archive Fever: A Freudian Impression." *Diacritics* 25, no. 2 (Summer 1995): 50.

18. Nicholas Feltron, "The 2010 Annual Report," accessed March 24, 2014, www.feltron.com/ar10_01.html. Other Feltron reports are autobiographical, but this report concerns his father and was occasioned by his passing in in September 2010: "The

2010 Annual Report is an encapsulation of my father's life, as communicated by the calendars, slides, and other artifacts in my possession."

19. Kathryn Math, unpublished essay, "As the Crow Flies: The Life of Warder Crow in Maps, Facts, and Statistical Data."

20. Jill Lepore, "Historians Who Love Too Much: Reflections on Microhistory and Biography," *Journal of American History* 88, no. 1 (June 2001): 133.

A Tale of Two Satterfields: The Power of a Purdue Education

 *Eden Holmes*

AT FIRST GLANCE, there is no discernible difference between the photographs of the two young men: similar dark hair with a deep side part, identically inquisitive gray eyes, matching stiff white collars, and indistinguishable solemn expressions.[1] No dissimilarities in their childhoods—the pair were born in rural West Virginia to large, humble farming families, attended the same two-room primary school and graduated from unpretentious Fairmont Normal School at the top of their respective classes.[2] Both men married women from their hometown, pursued higher education at personal expense, and fought to promote the working class in their professional lives.

Two notable people who sparked a researcher's nightmare. Two promising lads with the same name, born in the same year, in the same town. Only one difference existed in their youth, a difference that contributed to drastically divergent adulthoods: one attended Purdue.

Howard Ernest Satterfield and Howard Ernest Satterfield, twins in moniker and background, have caused me as their researcher to lose shattering amounts of sleep. I had been asked to create a biography of a Purdue student from the graduating class of 1904, and my research tracking Howard Satterfield, from Marion County, West Virginia, divulged no shortage of details, including an apparent four-year time gap where I assumed the young man was at Purdue. After weeks of in-depth research and drafting, I finally discovered the stressful truth—there were two men with matching monikers and a similar upbringing, and I had been tracing the path of the wrong one. I had confused the trails of their lives, mixed up by their identical names and similar backgrounds. However, after I began to examine their lives side by side, separating previously twisted strings of history and identifying the point of divergence—a Purdue education—I found the significance of the Boilermaker experience at the turn of the century. The youthful doppelgangers ultimately led starkly different lives after their identical childhood path diverged, and comparing their ultimate careers and lifestyles demonstrates the influence of a land-grant university education. Howard Ernest Satterfield, the Boilermaker (hereafter referred to as "the Professor"), and Howard Ernest Satterfield (henceforth denoted by "the Politician") embody an ideal contrast, as their remarkable (and confusing) similarities allow for perfect consideration of the results of a Purdue education on the life of a working-class young man.

The majority of university students at the turn of the twentieth century hailed from affluent families, whose financial stability enabled the students to focus solely upon schoolwork and social engagement during their time on campus. However, as land-grant institutions such as Purdue increasingly offered degrees in "practical" fields like engineering and agriculture, young people from varied backgrounds were beginning to seek higher education.[3] Such students, whose families struggled to fund their education, often worked their way through school, and their interactions with fellow, more affluent pupils were strained by class differences and economic contrasts.[4] The Professor, member of the Purdue class of 1904, financed his educational pursuits with an entrepreneurial tailoring business in West Lafayette, and my investigations into his life and the conditions of the institution during his schooling indicate that his pecuniary venture and modest upbringing placed the Professor on an alternate social plane from his classmates.[5]

As a land-grant college emerging from the Morrill Act of 1862, Purdue was founded on the principles of upward social mobility and educational equality, with the purpose of promoting "the liberal and practical education of the industrial classes in the several pursuits and professions in life . . . without excluding classical studies."[6] In order to support the development of the nation's industrial sector and facilitate agricultural progress, America built universities to educate engineers, agricultural experts, military specialists, and mechanical scientists, which differed from traditional collegiate curriculums that focused primarily on liberal arts and humanities. These universities, which included Cornell University, Massachusetts Institute of Technology, Clemson University, and numerous state institutions, offered achievable and practical educations in attempts to engage young people from diverse origins in academic achievement.[7]

Although these colleges existed to edify individuals in practical fields, the bulk of university students still hailed from privileged backgrounds, whose moneyed families were able to finance their scholarly pursuits, especially with the promise of financial return on their schooling.[8] Even individuals from traditional backgrounds, such as farming and modest service fields, usually had the financial means to enable the students to focus purely upon their education and social lives while at school. Education researchers Roger Geiger and Nathan Sorber argue that students from less advantaged backgrounds, such as the Professor, stuck out from their economically comfortable peers, as some pupils were forced to finance their own educations and restrained from pursuing the same social pursuits. Many had to drop their studies around harvest time, as they were needed at home, or stop school for a few semesters to earn their tuition for the next few.[9] In addition, the social engagements of young students, which include gambling, drinking, and fashion, stretched beyond the economic capabilities of working-class students, limiting their social equivalency to their peers. However, dedication to their studies and extracurricular engagement could allow a proletarian student a degree of social engagement, and their hard-won education expedited future success and achievement beyond their modest upbringings.

Born to humble farmers in West Virginia and obliged to support his family after the premature death of his father, the Professor's options for advanced education appeared grim.[10] During high school, he engaged in a brief apprenticeship to a tailor, indicating a youthful desire to pursue a modest lifestyle, although intelligence and effort afforded him dreams beyond clothes-making. His achievements in secondary school, where he graduated with a 98 percent grade average, earned him the opportunity to study beyond Fairmount State Normal School, but he was forced to bankroll his tuition during his tenure at Purdue. Many financially strapped students might have supplemented their meager income through dishwashing or other menial physical activity, but the Professor, in a rush of innovation and enterprise, launched his own tailoring business. He employed the skills gleaned from a rural childhood and an apprenticeship in tailoring to finance his pursuit of higher achievement.

The Professor advertised in numerous school and community newspapers, including the Purdue *Exponent*, promoting custom-made menswear and repair services for his classmates and teachers.[11] He was required to work alongside his studies, which may have demeaned him in the eyes of his peers. The Professor's customers were his fellow students, which may have made them—or him—feel he was in a subservient position. His frequent advertisements in the Purdue University newspaper, which engaged customers, also led to a possible social classification of "working class." Although his engagement brought him moderate success, his public image as a menial who was reliant on his contemporaries to remain in school likely impeded communication and community parity. The Professor was subjected to teasing and exposure from his fellow students, with jokes about his frequent advertisements appearing in his senior yearbook— "Satterfield Tries to Draw in Co-Ed Trade—Inquire Within."[12] In addition, his straight-arrow personality and aversion to financial waste were mocked, as a sarcastic poem rhymed, "What would you think if you should see . . . Satterfield playing poker?"[13] The Professor placed his academics (and paying for them) as his highest priority, and the hard work and dedication associated with such pursuits may have submitted him to rank suppression from his affluent peers, even as the institution's ideologies and administration worked to support diligent students from varied backgrounds.

Regardless of any social subjugation resulting from the Professor's background and value system, the young student still fought for equal recognition among his peers. Although he was teased and belittled, required to work long hours outside of the classroom, and limited by family circumstances, the Professor joined a fraternity, participated in the Masonic Society, and held the presidency of one of the most significant collegiate organizations at Purdue, the Young Men's Christian Association.[14] The Professor earned his bachelor's degree in mechanical engineering in less than four years, graduating with honors despite the pressures of maintaining his small business. The country boy from Nowheresville, West Virginia, battled the pressures of social stratification and the limitations of financial instability at Purdue University, and he went on to enjoy a lucrative career as an engineer and an academic.[15]

This education, received both from Purdue Engineering and the School of Hard Knocks, led the Professor through numerous manufacturing administration positions throughout the Midwest. Family tradition indicates that his burgeoning love of teaching, stemming from tenures as a night school educator held simultaneously with his jobs in manufacturing, resulted in a station as the head of the engineering departments at Winona Technical Institute in Indianapolis.[16] After a few years of marriage to his high school sweetheart, the first female graduate of the University of West Virginia, the Professor relocated his small family to North Carolina. He began his career in academia as an instructor of mechanical engineering at North Carolina State Agriculture and Mechanical College (now North Carolina State University), another land-grant institution.[17] The

Professor served as head of the department for decades, working as an advisor and mentor for a variety of young students.[18] Later, he began working as a contract engineer for numerous local business projects alongside his teaching position, applying his engineering knowledge to the practical pursuit of real estate construction.[19] Over 175 buildings in Raleigh held his neat sign, "Satterfield Built," and both positions—that of industrialist and instructor—contributed to his local prominence.[20] He maintained membership to the American Society of Mechanical Engineers and served as regional chief of the Engineering and Architectural Division of the Resettlement Administration.[21] Even in his esteemed rank as department chair, the Professor never failed to recognize the struggles of his working-class students, whose backgrounds mirrored his own. He hired several of his students who needed financial assistance to continue their educations to assist in his contracting jobs. Notable Raleigh businessman William Daniel Martin worked for his advisor, the Professor, during his entire term at the institution and later referred to him as an inspiration.[22]

The Professor reported that he owed his renown as an academic, engineer, and contractor to his education at Purdue University, where the collision of society with education helped to build his strength of conviction alongside the endowment of academic knowledge. He maintained ties to Purdue, returning to his alma mater numerous times to earn his master's degree in mechanical engineering and to receive the latest updates in his field. The University contributed to the Professor's early promotion and ultimate success, as the lessons bestowed during his stint at the institution greatly influenced the remainder of his professional and personal life.

But what would have happened if the Professor hadn't attended Purdue?

The Professor's archival twin, the identically named Howard Ernest Satterfield, the Politician, demonstrates a contrasting fate. When the Professor departed for college in Indiana, the Politician remained in their small West Virginia town, and the course of his life indicates the possible resulting course of a non-Boilermaker.

The second Satterfield, the Politician, began life as a middle child of eleven, working on the family farm at the expense of a secondary education.[23] Rather than pursue an advanced degree, the Politician lingered in the Fairmont area after high school graduation, working assorted jobs as a miner, meat-cutter, and grocery clerk, none of which engaged the intellectual prowess demonstrated by his notable academic scores in primary school. After starting a family with his own high school sweetheart, the Politician completed a mail course in law from the American Correspondence School in Chicago presumably in the hopes of furthering his status, but he remained in rural Marion County, pursuing various careers as a meat-packing manager, insurance salesman, and auctioneer.[24] His modest achievement provided financial comfort for his wife and six children, but as the Professor's career suggests, the Politician was continually outpaced by his more academically accomplished competitors in career success and community acknowledgment.

In each of his diverse vocations, the Politician may have noted the same drastic social stratification that had plagued his doppelganger, observing the stark contrasts of treatment, pay, and prospects of individuals based upon their background and educational experiences. However, rather than working within the education system to build academic foundations, the Politician sought to implement change through the civil sphere. After earning a seat in the West Virginia State House of Representatives in the early 1920s, the Politician served on the Committee of Arts, Sciences, and General Improvements, where many of his extant speeches describe the importance of propagating applicable scientific and engineering knowledge.[25] State documentation in the early 1930s indicates the Politician's personal ties to the working class, as he called upon the legislature to regulate the conditions and pay for West Virginian coal miners. In spite of the rank suppression reinforced by his job-hopping years, eventually Satterfield achieved a degree of status as a politician in one of the poorer counties of West Virginia, working to support and promote blue-collar employees until his death.[26] While the social restrictions of his background impeded his personal success, the Politician later utilized the lessons acquired in his work experience to champion others standing in his shoes.

At the beginning of the twentieth century, the chaos of development caused numerous class conflicts and facilitated incredible social stratification, as blue-collar individuals sought to participate in the upward social mobility promised by increased educational opportunities. The pair of Satterfields, almost mirror images in childhood, familial background, and intellectual potential, were divided by a college education, an academic pursuit followed by one and missed by the other. Although their initial capabilities shone identically, the sacrifices made by the Professor in the pursuit of a Purdue diploma later contributed to distinguished achievement in scholarly and engineering fields, while the Politician struggled for years to achieve recognition of his intellectual skills in the political realm due to his unstable background and lack of an academic degree. In the changing world of the early 1900s, a Purdue University education represented ability, knowledge, and experience. A working-class student's diligence in the classroom and at his side job paved the way for an active transition from farm boy to college department chair. Although the difficulties of social subjugation and rank pressures constricted the growth of the twain Howard Ernest Satterfields, the Purdue experience facilitated an academic livelihood for the Professor, who continued to support the education of other working-class students for decades.

Bibliography

American Society of Mechanical Engineers. *List of Members*. New York: The Society, 1909.

Association of Land-Grant and Public Universities. *The Land-Grant Tradition*. Washington, DC: Association of Land-Grant and Public Universities, 2012. http://www.aplu.org/document.doc?id=780.

Gieger, Roger L., and Nathan M. Sorber. *The Land-Grant Colleges and the Reshaping of American Higher Education*. Piscataway: Transaction Publishers, 2013.

Gilchrist Gibson Satterfield, Frances. *From Whence We Came*. Raleigh: Itek Method Addressing Duplicating Service, 1973.

Hall, Richard. "North Carolina Modernist Houses—America's Largest Archive of Residential Modernist Design." North Carolina Modernist Houses: Documenting, Preserving, and Promoting Residential Modernist Architecture. Last modified November 6, 2013. http://www.trianglemodernisthouses.com/raleigh.htm.

Martin, Jr., William D. "William D. Martin." J. T. Martin. n.d. http://jtmartinonline.com/documents/New28-Martin,Buck-WD.htm.

North Carolina College of Agriculture and Mechanic Arts. *Agricultural and Mechanical College Record*. Raleigh: The College, 1911.

North Carolina Department of State Auditor. *Annual Report of the Auditor of the State*. Raleigh: North Carolina Department of State, 1922.

Purdue *Debris*. 1904. The Virginia Kelly Karnes Archives and Special Collections Research Center, Purdue University Libraries.

Raleigh Historic Development Commission. "Hayes Barton Historic District." Raleigh Historic Development Commission. Last modified September 7, 2012. http://www.rhdc.org/hayes-barton-historic-district.

Reef, Catherine. *Education and Learning in America*. New York: Infobase Publishing, 2009.

Satterfield, Howard E. "Student Merchant Tailor." *Exponent* (West Lafayette, IN), Sept. 30, 1903.

———. "Suits and Overcoats." *Exponent* (West Lafayette, IN), Nov. 11, 1903.

United States Bureau of Education. *Bulletin*. Washington, DC: United States Government Printing Office, 1917.

United States Data Repository. *Howard Ernest Satterfield*. Washington, DC: United States Genealogy Network, 1922. http://www.us-data.org/wv/marion/bios/satterfield_howard-ernest_1885-1969.txt.

United States Office of Education. *Bulletin*. Washington, DC: United States Department of Health, Education, and Welfare, 1918.

United States Senate. 37th Congress, 2nd Session. *S-130, An Act Donating Public Lands to the Several States and Territories which may Provide Colleges for the Benefit of Agriculture and the Mechanic Arts*. Washington, DC: Government Printing Office, 1862.

West Virginia Division of Culture and History. *West Virginia Legislators: Marion County*. West Virginia Archives and History, 2013. http://www.wvculture.org/history/government/legislature/legislatorsmarion.html.

West Virginia Legislature. *West Virginia Blue Book*. Charleston: West Virginia Senate Clerk's Office, 1922.

Notes

1. The photographs I describe come from: Frances Gilchrist Gibson Satterfield, *From Whence We Came* (Raleigh: Itek Method Addressing Duplicating Service, 1973), 180, and West Virginia Legislature, *West Virginia Blue Book* (Charleston: West Virginia Senate Clerk's Office, 1922), 152.

2. *Debris*, 1904, the Virginia Kelly Karnes Archives and Special Collections Research Center, Purdue University Libraries, 108.

3. Association of Land-Grant and Public Universities, *The Land-Grant Tradition* (Washington, DC: Association of Land-Grant and Public Universities, 2012), 9. These "practical" degrees pre-dated the land-grant university system, existing for centuries, but the incorporation of agriculture and engineering into standard curricula at land-grant universities facilitated the ability of the average individual to obtain a degree.

4. Catherine Reef, *Education and Learning in America* (New York: Infobase Publishing, 2009), 96–97. Reef identifies the difficulties of the university experience for working-class students, who, in the attempt to achieve an education to better their futures, were faced with financial and class barriers to social acceptance among their wealthier classmates.

5. Advertisement written by Howard E. Satterfield, "Suits and Overcoats," *Exponent* (West Lafayette, IN), Nov. 11, 1903.

6. Quotation of from the text of the Morrill Land-Grant Act, originating from the United States Senate, 37th Congress, 2nd Session, *S-130, An Act Donating Public Lands to the Several States and Territories which may Provide Colleges for the Benefit of Agriculture and the Mechanic Arts* (Washington: Government Printing Office, 1862).

7. Affiliations of specific universities as land-grant universities is found in Association of Land-Grant and Public Universities, *The Land-Grant Tradition* (Washington, DC: Association of Land-Grant and Public Universities, 2012), 14.

8. Roger L. Gieger and Nathan M. Sorber, *The Land-Grant Colleges and the Reshaping of American Higher Education* (Piscataway: Transaction Publishers, 2013), 159.

9. Ibid., 167.

10. Frances Gilchrist Gibson Satterfield, *From Whence We Came* (Raleigh: Itek Method Addressing Duplicating Service, 1973), 178.

11. Howard E. Satterfield, "Student Merchant Tailor," *Exponent* (West Lafayette, IN), Sept. 30, 1903, 24.

12. *Debris*, 1904, 293. Although such teasing and jibing was common among students at Purdue during the time period, the majority of references to Satterfield in school publications focused upon other students' critiques of his humbler background and resulting financial thriftiness and dedication of character.

13. Ibid., 300.

14. Ibid., 108.

15. Howard Ernest Satterfield was technically from Marion County, West Virginia, not "Nowheresville," although the rural area likely felt like the middle of nowhere on occasion.

16. Gibson Satterfield, *From Whence We Came*, 356.

17. North Carolina College of Agriculture and Mechanic Arts, *Agricultural and Mechanical College Record* (Raleigh: The College, 1911). North Carolina Department of State Auditor, *Annual Report of the Auditor of the State* (Raleigh: North Carolina Department of State, 1922).

18. United States Bureau of Education, *Bulletin* (Washington, DC: United States Government Printing Office, 1917), 96. United States Office of Education, *Bulletin* (Washington, DC: United States Department of Health, Education, and Welfare, 1918), 131.

19. Richard Hall, "North Carolina Modernist Houses— America's Largest Archive of Residential Modernist Design," *North Carolina Modernist Houses: Documenting, Preserving, and*

Promoting Residential Modernist Architecture, last modified November 6, 2013. Raleigh Historic Development Commission, "Hayes Barton Historic District," *Raleigh Historic Development Commission*, last modified September 7, 2012.

20. Gibson Satterfield, *From Whence We Came*, 358.

21. American Society of Mechanical Engineers, *List of Members* (New York: The Society, 1909), 162.

22. William D. Martin Junior, "William D. Martin" (J. T. Martin, n.d.).

23. United States Data Repository, *Howard Ernest Satterfield* (Washington, DC: The United States Genealogy Network, 1922).

24. West Virginia Legislature, *West Virginia Blue Book* (Charleston: West Virginia Senate Clerk's Office, 1922), 152.

25. West Virginia Division of Culture and History, *West Virginia Legislators: Marion County* (West Virginia Archives and History, 2013).

26. United States Data Repository, *Howard Ernest Satterfield* (Washington, DC: The United States Genealogy Network, 1922).

"The Only Colored Drug Store": Richard Wirt Smith's Success Story, 1904–1911

Maggie Mace

In 1905, Smith & Co. was a thriving, new business located in the heart of Indianapolis, Indiana. An African American man, Richard Wirt Smith owned this pharmacy store. The racial disparities of the early twentieth century did not slow Richard down, but encouraged him to open his business just a year after graduating from Purdue University. Indianapolis was one of the few cities in which African Americans were allowed out past dark, making the city attractive to them. Richard was an active member of this community and regularly advertised in the *Indianapolis Recorder*, a newspaper created for the African

American community, in which he claimed that his business, Smith & Co., was the "only colored drug store" around the Indianapolis area. His dedication and success led him to a prestigious lifestyle that he enjoyed until he enlisted for military service during WWI. His experiences are a window into the racial climate of the period. In this chapter I trace Richard's accomplishments as a young man from the time of his graduation in 1904 until 1911, the year he was married and entered a new phase of his life.

Richard graduated with a bachelor's degree in pharmacy in 1904 from Purdue University. There were two hundred and thirty seniors that year, and thirty-six of them were pharmacy students. There were not many students in Purdue's pharmacy program, however, because it had been recently created in 1894. Richard was just one of two African American students in the 1904 graduating class. Slavery had been abolished just forty years prior and segregation was still strong; therefore, African American enrollment was extremely low. Richard was not allowed to live on campus or in West Lafayette, because he was an African American student.[1] All African American students who attended Purdue during the early 1900s had to live over the bridge until the 1940s.

Most of the men who attended Purdue during this time were involved in different organizations, clubs, and fraternities, but Richard was not. This could have been because he was not allowed to be involved due to his color, or he just simply chose not to be involved. Neither of the African American students in this class had any extracurricular activities listed in the Purdue 1904 *Debris*.[2] The short biography written next to Richard's picture in the *Debris* does mention "he is the best baseball player in the class and has had considerable experience along that line."[3] It is not specified whether he participated with the class club baseball team or the school varsity baseball team. If Smith was on the actual varsity team, he was never listed on the roster or pictured with Purdue's baseball team during his time at Purdue. His picture and information regarding baseball might not be in the *Debris* because he could have been absent on picture day, or the students who ran the *Debris* and student organizations discriminated against him due to his race. The evidence is not conclusive; the lack of involvement could be a coincidence or personal choice, or it could indicate the early struggles of African American students.

A passage from a letter to the editor in the Purdue *Exponent* in the section labeled "Was it 'Gentlemanly'?" leads me to believe that he was not on Purdue's varsity team. The letter was written in support of white students at Purdue who had yelled racial taunts at an African American player on the Beloit College team who had come to West Lafayette for an away game. The letter says, "Let us ask the question—does a Negro belong on the football team of any white man's school? No! Football is a white man's game and let us play it, as Purdue does, with white men."[4] If a sentiment existed among students that African Americans should not play on "their" football team, then it is difficult to believe that white students would allow an African American to play on their baseball team. The only reason his baseball skills were probably documented at all in the *Debris* was because the students created their fellow peers' biographies. It is possible that his classmates noticed his fantastic playing skills and sought to recognize them, although he did not play on the varsity team.

Richard's peers apparently thought it was vital to add that he was somewhat of a "buttinsky" in his *Debris* biography. A buttinsky, or a buttinski, is someone who gets involved with other people's business.[5] It is possible that they called Richard a buttinsky because of his color and thought he was an intruder at a predominantly white college. On the other hand, the *Debris* editors could have known him well enough to tease him. There is no evidence to show that he was subject to direct racial discrimination, but this label does tell that he was considered a pushy character.

Attending Purdue during this time was a great advantage for African American students because few of them enrolled in college, and especially not colleges that were almost exclusively white. As the Library of Congress exhibit "America at School" explains, "After 1900, as more African Americans achieved a high school education, high schools gradually took on the ideals of the 'common' school that elementary schools had espoused. Typically only the middle or upper classes could afford to send their children to college or university."[6] Attending college gave Richard a chance to live the American dream. His decision to pursue pharmacy set him apart from the other students, since the program was fairly new to the University and the majority of Purdue students studied engineering and agriculture. Richard chose a very prestigious major for the time period, and his endeavor paid off.

In figure 1, a picture of one of Purdue's pharmacy classes, we see Richard located in almost the very center of the picture. I would expect him to be toward the back or near a corner based on my assumptions about racism at Purdue during this time period. His centrality is almost ironic, since he was mentioned as a buttinsky in his *Debris* excerpt, and here we find him in the middle of all of his fellow classmates. This depiction hints at the somewhat confusing relationship between African American students and their white counterparts of the time period. Although history often suggests that discrimination was strong in such situations, evidence, such as the pharmacy photo, shows African American students may have been close and comfortable with classmates.

Figure 1. Richard pictured center (*Debris* 1904, 56).

Born in Indianapolis on September 27, 1884, Richard moved back to his hometown after graduation, where he would live the rest of his life. Richard's pharmacy degree took him far in life, considering that a lot of African Americans during this time did not experience great success and usually did not have good paying, steady jobs.[7] Between the years of 1894 to 1915 most African Americans were also generally limited in their work opportunities. According to "America at Work," "In Northern cities, African Americans generally held a better economic position than did their Southern peers. Still, their options were limited, as the majority performed labor or service work. Common occupations for men were janitors, servants, and waiters. Women were housekeepers, servants, laundresses, and waitresses."[8]

Shortly after graduation, Richard beat the odds by opening Smith & Co. His business was located in the greater African American community of Indianapolis. Richard appears to have lived above his pharmacy during the first couple years after it opened. His business, along with several other African American-owned businesses, was on Senate Avenue.[9] The African American community had its own groceries, churches, barbers, theaters, restaurants, drug stores, pharmacies, clothing stores, and so forth, and Richard's pharmacy was an important part of the district.

Indianapolis was a popular city for African Americans, because it was one of the areas where African Americans could be out after dark and actually live as full citizens. By contrast, there were several cities surrounding Indianapolis in which people of color could not stay out after dark. James Loewen, the author of *Sundown Towns: A Hidden Dimension of American Racism*, says, "From Maine to California, thousands of communities kept out African Americans (or sometimes Chinese Americans, Jewish Americans, etc.) by force, law, or custom. These communities are sometimes called 'sundown towns' because some of them posted signs at their city limits reading, typically, 'Nigger, Don't Let The Sun Go Down On You In ___.'"[10]

Since Indianapolis did not enact a similar law, the city became somewhat of a safe haven for African American people. The city's acceptance of the population allowed African Americans, and Richard, to build a strong and active community that was uncommon for the time. The strength and success of the community was well documented by a local newspaper.

In addition to the *Indianapolis Recorder*, the city also had two other African American weekly newspapers, the *Freeman* and the *World*. The *Indianapolis Recorder* kept the African American community extremely close and informed, which helped create a strong bond. The newspaper reported on politics, elections, celebrations, and meetings in the African American community. The *Indianapolis Recorder* usually ranged from about four to eight pages of information regarding the African American community.

Underneath the title was its motto: "A Weekly Newspaper Devoted to the Best Interests of the Negroes of Indiana." The *Indianapolis Recorder* was not only focused on the greater Indianapolis area, but also the entire state of Indiana. There are notes from each city in Indiana that discuss various occurences.[11] In this way, the wider African American communities were able to support and know each other.

Although Indianapolis was progressive by the standards of the time, it was by no means a perfect union. Carolyn Brady writes, "Although some white-owned businesses did solicit black customers by advertising in the *Recorder*, many other white storekeepers and restaurant and theater owners refused to serve African Americans or attempted to drive them away by rude treatment or inflated prices."[12] Consequently during this time, African Americans only patronized African American businesses, and the whites patronized white businesses. Therefore, although not legally mandated, segregation still existed and each group experienced separate success. The majority of African Americans were new to the Indianapolis area from the South. The surge of African Americans wanted their own businesses to grow and succeed, and this spirit effectively strengthened Indianapolis.

A lot of the newspaper space was used for advertisements of all of the African American-owned businesses. Richard put out several advertisements in the *Indianapolis Recorder* promoting his pharmacy on North Senate Avenue. Many of the advertisements Richard placed in the newspaper publicized different medicines that he carried, how genuine his business was (he would "give money back if unsatisfied"), and his claims that his was the only "colored drug store" in Indianapolis.[13] One of the first advertisements Richard ever put in the newspaper in 1905 reads, "Stop, for constipation and all stomach troublers take California Prune Wafers. A sure cure guaranteed or money refunded. R. W. Smith Pharmacist. 13 Senate Avenue."[14] The line that caught my eye is "or money refunded." Smith was aware of standard business practices early on in his career. And more, the advertisement perhaps shows that African Americans were looking out for each other and cared about their community.

In 1907, about two and a half years after Richard opened his business, he attended what seems to be a very important meeting. The *Indianapolis Recorder* published a list of several people around the state who were part of a program to be held at Jones Tabernacle, an Indianapolis church. The article's headline read, "A Great Meeting, Business Men of Indiana to Organize State League, Attendance Will Be Large—Interesting Program to be Presented."[15] The mayor of Indianapolis, Charles A. Bookwalter, was at this important meeting for the businessmen and women of Indianapolis. The African American community had extremely successful businesses; the white mayor would not have come to open the meeting if businesses were not thriving. Richard was at this meeting representing his pharmacy. Richard not only attended the meeting, but he also spoke about his business. There were several other African American business owners present who all gave speeches. Many different businesses were represented, such as a barbershop, market, garden business, tailor, hair salon, and a confectionary store. This again speaks to the strength of the Indianapolis African American community.

Another advertisement Richard placed in the *Indianapolis Recorder* said, "Greatest care used, and pure drugs only. The only colored drug store in Indy. Your trade is solicited on Merit. Cor. Senate Ave & 13th Street. New phone 410."[16] This particular advertisement is an interesting source of information for two reasons. First, Richard claims that he is the "only colored drug store" in his area, which means his business faced little competition and African Americans with pharmacy degrees were a rarity. Also, Richard must have bought a telephone for his booming business. Fortunately, Richard's business was doing well enough for him to afford a telephone. Purchasing the telephone may have changed the rest of his career, because he now had access to quicker business communication that he lacked before. A lot of the other businesses advertised in the *Indianapolis Recorder* listed that they had telephones as well. His telephone purchase kept him up-to-date with the other local business practices. It also gave him more of an advantage, since, as he again claimed, he was operating the "only colored drug store" in Indianapolis. On the other hand, during my research I kept seeing another druggist's advertisements in the *Indianapolis Reporter* promoting the Carter Rheumatic Cure, although Richard said he was the "only colored drug store" in Indy. It is unclear if the other advertised druggist sold different types of medications, if he was in a city other than Indianapolis, or if the other pharmacy was a white-owned business interested in attracting African American customers.

In 1911, Richard's life changed once again. As the *Indianapolis Recorder* noted, "Richard Wirt Smith, the pharmacist, and Miss Dove Bertha Barbour, a teacher in the public school were quietly married at noon, June 20. Only the relatives and several intimate friends were present. Mr. and Mrs. Smith will be at home to their friends, at 622 Drake Street."[17] Dove was a schoolteacher in the greater Indianapolis area, but she soon resigned after their marriage.[18] The *Indianapolis Recorder* suggests that Richard and Dove were actively involved with the African American community. They both attended important meetings to benefit themselves and the community as a whole. They were a spiritual couple, meaning they attended church and found it important to live by the word of God. Dove attended concerts, benefits, and gatherings that took place in the churches throughout the African American community.

Over the next few years, Richard still had a few advertisements published in the *Indianapolis Recorder*, but the archival trail runs cold after this point. It is known that he registered for military service on September 12, 1918, but I have not been able to locate any service records.[19] If he did serve, his return to Indianapolis may have been difficult. When African American veterans came back from war, relationships between them and the whites was not in good standing. Sadly, a lot of returning African Americans were murdered and lynched. The war was almost over by 1918, so one wonders why he decided to register so late. During a few months of 1918, men were drafted into the war, which could have been the reason Richard registered.

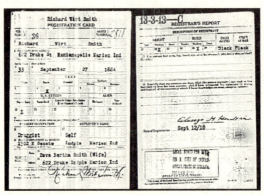

Figure 2. Richard's registration card (ancestry.com).

Perhaps his business began to suffer, and his solution was to move on and serve his country.

Whatever the reason for his registration, from this point on I have been unable to locate more information about him. More information about Richard's success and community involvement awaits a time when I or someone else can continue to pursue the topic. There are many more questions that could be asked. Richard Wirt Smith lived a very successful life even though circumstances were difficult for African American men in this time period. Although his life story as chronicled by this chapter is incomplete, what we do know speaks to the climate of the time. Smith's experiences as a university student and practicing professional show that African Americans were making gains at the turn on the twentieth century. Furthermore, Indianapolis's liberal approach to African American integration appears to have in fact boosted the city. The community worked very hard to be as successful as possible. Finally, much of Richard's good fortune can be accredited to his pharmacy degree that he earned from Purdue University in 1904. If he had not had a college education, I am not sure how far life would have taken him. In whatever way Richard left this world, I am confident he left in peace.

Bibliography

"A Great Meeting." *Indianapolis Recorder*, July 27, 1907.

Advertisement for Pharmacy. *Indianapolis Recorder*, February 25, 1905.

———. *Indianapolis Recorder*, February 29, 1908.

"America at School." *Library of Congress*. http://memory.loc.gov/ammem/awlhtml/awlscho.html.

"America at Work." *Library of Congress*. http://memory.loc.gov/ammem/awlhtml/awlwork.html.

Brady, Carolyn. "Indianapolis and the Great Migration, 1900-1920." C. M. Brady, 1996. http://www.carolynbrady.com/indymigration.html.

"In Club Circles." *Indianapolis Recorder*, June 24, 1911.

Indianapolis Recorder, May 5, 1906.

Loewen, James W. *Sundown Towns: A Hidden Dimension of American Racism*. New York: The New Press, 2005.

Merriam-Webster On-Line, s.v. "buttinsky," http://www.merriam-webster.com/dictionary/buttinsky.

Purdue *Debris*. 1904. The Virginia Kelly Karnes Archives and Special Collections Research Center, Purdue University Libraries.

"Was It 'Gentlemanly'?" *Exponent* (West Lafayette, IN), Oct. 7, 1903.

"Resignations." *Indianapolis Star*, June 15, 1912.

Smith, Richard Wirt. Registration card, September 12, 1918. Ancestry.com. *U.S. World War I Draft Registration Cards, 1917-1918* (Provo, Utah: Ancestry.com Operations), 2005.

Notes

1. His address while attending Purdue was documented as 223 Main Street. 223 Main Street is now a Downtown Bar and Pub named the Black Sparrow.

2. It's illuminating to compare Smith to some of the white students who were involved while on campus. Irwin Emory Artz's affiliations were listed as "Sigma Alpha Epsilon; Tau Beta Pi, Wilbur Scholarship; *Debris* Staff, Advertising Manager." Another white student, Roger Victor Brewster's affiliations read "Civil Engineering Society; Class Baseball Team; Minstrels; Band; Athletics."

3. *Debris*, 1904, 110.

4. "Was It 'Gentlemanly'?," *Exponent* (West Lafayette, IN), Oct. 7, 1903.

5. *Merriam-Webster On-Line*, s.v. "buttinsky," http://www.merriam-webster.com/dictionary/buttinsky.

6. "America at School," *Library of Congress*, http://memory.loc.gov/ammem/awlhtml/awlscho.html.

7. "America at Work," *Library of Congress*, http://memory.loc.gov/ammem/awlhtml/awlwork.html.

8. "America at School."

9. His business is longer there. 1301 North Senate Avenue is now an intersection in the Downtown area.

10. James W. Loewen, *Sundown Towns: A Hidden Dimension of American Racism* (2005). This book talks about all of the Sundown Towns in the United States during this time.

11. Advertisement for Pharmacy, *Indianapolis Recorder*, Feb. 25, 1905, 2.

12. The passage continues, "Indiana's civil rights law of 1885 stated that places of public accommodation had to serve all people 'regardless of race,' but African Americans who tried to challenge discriminatory practices in court could lose when judges resorted to very literal interpretations of the law." Originally published in C. M. Brady, "Indianapolis and The Great Migration, 1900-1920," *Black History News & Notes* 65 (Aug. 1996), http://www.carolynbrady.com/indymigration.html.

13. A note from the city of Lafayette on May 12, 1906, said, "R. Wirt Smith of Indianapolis was in the city this week." "Lafayette," *Indianapolis Recorder*, May 5, 1906, 3.

14. Advertisement for Pharmacy, *Indianapolis Recorder*, Feb. 25, 1905, 2.

15. "A Great Meeting," *Indianapolis Recorder*, July 27, 1907, 1.

16. Advertisement for Pharmacy. *Indianapolis Recorder*, Feb. 29, 1908, 4.

17. "In Club Circles," *Indianapolis Recorder,* June 24, 1911, 4.
18. "Resignations." *Indianapolis Star,* June 15, 1912, 11.
19. Richard Wirt Smith, Registration card, September 12, 1918, Ancestry.com, *U.S. World War I Draft Registration Cards, 1917-1918* (Provo, Utah: Ancestry.com Operations), 2005.

Emil Farkas and William Raymond Davis: Windy City Boys

Emily Durkin

It was a crisp autumn day in the windy city. The year was 1902, and Emil braced himself against the cold Chicago wind as he made his way to civil engineering class at the Armour Institute, thinking that things needed to change. Maybe he needed a change of pace; this city wasn't offering the opportunities he sought. While the Armour Institute was a respected technical institute, perhaps he needed a place that could offer a more prestigious kind of education. Maybe the city life was not for him. What about a school that was on the verge of growth? What about Purdue University in West Lafayette?

In another part of the city, William Raymond Davis was having thoughts similar to Emil's, but with different motivations. Chicago for him had meant tragedy. Maybe this was the reason he wanted to leave the Chicago Manual Training School.[1] Purdue could be a fresh start, William thought. He could escape the past and start anew.

But would the country boys in West Lafayette accept these city boys?

Purdue University was becoming a renowned institution for its engineering and agricultural programs at the turn of the twentieth century. Through Emil Farkas and William Raymond Davis, both transfer students to Purdue who graduated in 1904, we explore the role of the Chicagoan in a rural setting and the extent to which the rural and urban divide shaped life at the turn of the century. The archival trail of these two young men is almost nonexistent. The legacies of both men remain fragmented and incomplete—ghosts of the past. Their trails ran cold early in my archival research, and the records of their experiences at Purdue are minimal. Much about their lives is left to speculation at the turn of the twentieth century.

According to Timothy Spears, professor of American Studies at Middlebury College and author of *Chicago Dreaming: Midwesterners and the City, 1871–1919*, "Even today, the lure of the city remains a potent theme in American popular culture; part of a familiar narrative about leaving home and starting over, they also underscore the culture's abiding faith in the relationship between physical and social mobility, a belief powered, and challenged, by a variety of desires and longings."[2] It may have been this sentiment and the opportunities that the city provided that drew Emil's parents to the United States from Austria in 1889 when Emil was only six years old.[3] This move to a new country and learning an entirely new language may have had a severe impact on Emil. At that time, Americans were generally not accepting of immigrants, and they were led to believe immigrants were taking away American jobs and spoiling the American name. Emil and his parents moved to Chicago instead of a rural town, such as West Lafayette, as was commonly the case with immigrants, due to the nature of the rural and urban divide. Chicago had a large German-speaking population at that time, as Spears explains: "Among the city's older immigrant communities, the Germans were the largest, totaling a quarter of the entire population."[4] While the city was no friendly place for immigrants, the rural setting was far worse. The city needed immigrants to create the cultural melting pot it is today.[5] Emil's experiences living in Chicago as an immigrant may have shaped the course of his life. The Chicago immigrant community was overcrowded with poorly constructed housing. The German community in particular seemed to congregate on the near north side of Chicago.[6] These early experiences may have played a role for Emil in his development and eventual determination to find a better life than the one he was dealt.

On the other hand, William Raymond Davis, a native of Blue Island, Illinois—a suburb of Chicago—had immigrant parents as well, yet his experiences seem to have been starkly different than Emil's.[7] William's archival trail has substantially more information than Emil's.

William's parents, William Thomas Davis and Frances Davis, were born and raised in England. According to an 1871 marriage record from Grimsby, England, William Thomas Davis married Frances Reynolds.[8] The Davises immigrated to Chicago perhaps because of the perceived endless opportunities afforded to those who moved to the city. However, the experience of an English immigrant speaking with an accent was easier than the experience of an

Austrian immigrant incapable of being understood, as he spoke only German. One can only speculate as to how the two young men's lives played out in the various stages of childhood since no archival records exist. It is known that both young men grew up in the ever-changing city of Chicago with many opportunities for advancement. The city could also be a place to lose oneself. Our experiences shape who we are, and William especially experienced much tragedy in his life. It is this tragedy that may have led him to flee Chicago for a "new life" at Purdue University. William experienced the death of his mother at the age of forty-two in 1892, his older brother Walter Davis in 1898, and his brother Fred Davis.[9] The deaths of these family members may have prompted him to leave the Chicago Manual Training School.[10] While the school was a respected institution, it may not have offered William enough opportunities to advance his career. Purdue was a four-year institution, and to be the best in his field, William may have needed to transfer to pursue better educational standards. The Purdue name may have drawn the city boy to the small-town, land-grant institution of West Lafayette.

While the city of Chicago was booming, the rural setting was also undergoing change. In their study of changing demographics, Daniel Lichter and David

Brown found that "in 1900, more than 60% of Americans lived in rural areas, defined as small towns, the open countryside, and farms."[11] The small-town setting was one where common American ideals, such as hard work and religious morals, flourished. The city was typically viewed as impersonal and immoral. According to issues of the Purdue *Exponent*, students at the University poked fun at rural areas like Kansas and implied that West Lafayette and the greater Purdue community considered itself to have a higher status than such areas. This is evidenced through a 1904 issue of the *Exponent* with an aside that states, "Piano playing is prohibited in Forb Scott, Kansas between the hours of 10 p.m. and 7 a.m. It interferes with the engagement of the sound made by the corn growing."[12] However much Purdue students wanted to see themselves as urban and sophisticated, for Chicagoans, West Lafayette must have seemed simple. The struggle between the urban and rural divide is evident in Emil's senior biographical excerpt, published in the 1904 *Debris*. In Emil's brief biography, it is implied that Emil could not stop talking about his days at the Armour Institute before transferring to Purdue. Perhaps Emil mentioned the Armour Institute in excess because he missed Chicago and the experiences it offered. Often, the past is idealized, and memories make one nostalgic. Emil may have yearned for his years at Armour because of a deep connection he felt with Chicago as his adopted hometown. Spears argues that immigrants felt this way about their original homes: "One marker of provincial migrants' identity in Chicago, nostalgia was a socially constructed emotion that referred primarily to geographic dislocation and the longing for home that followed."[13] It is possible that "immigrants" to Purdue from Chicago transferred their nostalgia to the city. It can be noted that no matter where one comes from, one will long for home. Emil's longing is duly noted by others in their description of him: "of course he is from Chicago."[14] Transplants from Chicago to Indiana can identify with Emil and his longing for that great Windy City. I can speak to his desire for talking of home and the great opportunities Chicago offers as I am a Chicagoan myself. This repeated mention in Emil's senior *Debris* biography suggests Emil's motivation to transfer to Purdue. While Chicago may have offered many positive experiences and memories of the past, the Purdue name as a large land-grant institution was becoming well-known for its engineering program, which may have been what brought Emil to West Lafayette. What did Emil expect coming to Purdue? Were his expectations based on rural and "farm boy" stereotypes? What was William's motivation to transfer to Purdue? Was it the growing reputation of Purdue and its engineering program?

While both students have similar trajectories, stark differences exist between them. Emil seemingly disappears while at Purdue. There is only mention of him in a poem regarding the graduating seniors of the class of 1904.[15] Surprisingly, he does have an extended biography in the *Debris* from 1904. Other than this moment in the *Debris*, he appears to leave no trace of himself while at Purdue in terms of his school involvement and active memberships. William, however, took a different path and became involved in the Athletic Association as well as the Mechanical Engineering Society, according to the 1904 *Debris*.[16] William neither fades into the background at Purdue nor stands out strongly. Why did these two young men have such low profiles while at the University? What caused the lack of archival information that suggests such minimal involvement? Their low profiles might be the result of the lack of archival information, or their obscurity might stem from the difficulty of transferring and coming to a class that had already bonded.

It was another windy autumn day in 1903; it was the Windy City boys' senior year. Purdue was bustling with students moving in, greeting old friends, and getting back into the swing of academic life. This academic year would be marked with traditions, such as the annual tank scrap, and the tragedy of the horrific train wreck.[17] Another commonality that exists between the two young men occurs later in this year. From 1903 to 1904, their senior year at Purdue, each Chicagoan wrote his senior thesis on the topic of Chicago and engineering. According to the 1904 *Debris*, Emil wrote his senior thesis on the tunnel under the Chicago River, and William wrote his on the design of special steel under-framing for Pullman cars that originated in Chicago, which back then was the transportation hub it still is today.[18] This implies that Chicago remained a fascination for both men, despite their transfers to Purdue University.

These men were leading lives with similar trajectories, and it is with these similarities and differences that we can explore the rural and urban divide. In both young men's experiences, which were recorded in excerpts written about them, it appears that they were set apart from other students because they transferred to Purdue from a big city. The question arises as to why the city and rural areas have been in conflict. Are the two areas so ideologically different that they cannot come to accept one another? As Spears argues, "In the starkest of terms, the taboo pleasures of urban culture were opposed to the virtues of rural life."[19] This quote illustrates the stereotypical differences that divide urban and rural settings. It was believed at the time that the urban setting was filled with squalor and temptation, while the rural setting was filled with rolling fields and strict morality. It may explain why Emil and William could have felt different from the other students while at Purdue.

Both young men went their own ways in life, and there is no evidence that either had any contact with one another while at Purdue University. Both men married and had families, as discovered through census and *Ancestry.com* research. Emil fought for a better life for himself and his family, and he went on to be the father of two sons.[20] He fought hard to break out of his status as an immigrant. According to the 1930 US federal census, Emil worked in advertising, and the Farkas family eventually had a servant.[21] William appears in the Purdue Alumni Directory, while Emil does not.[22] William chose to pursue a career as a mechanical engineer and traveled to the West Coast, landing in Douglas, Arizona, to work for numerous railroad and mining companies.[23] The ties between Purdue and Chicago that these two men had still exist today. Many Purdue students travel to the city of Chicago for fun day trips or educational purposes.[24] What were the motivational factors for these two young men to transfer, move back home to the great Windy City, or forge on with their lives elsewhere? One can only speculate, and the circumstances are situational. The Chicago ties and rural connection to Purdue bound these "city boys" together even if they didn't know it. Emil Farkas and William Raymond Davis offer a snapshot of the Purdue University setting at the turn of the twentieth century, as well as the tensions of the day between rural and urban centers. Despite the fact that the lives of both young men diverged, one thread remains constant: no matter where they went in life, Chicago would always be their home.

Bibliography

Brown, David, and Daniel Lichter. "Rural America in an Urban Society: Changing Spatial and Social Boundaries." *Annual Review of Sociology* 566, no. 37 (2011).

Bulletin of Purdue University. Purdue Alumni Registry. The Virginia Kelly Karnes Archives and Special Collections Research Center, Purdue University Libraries. West Lafayette, IN, 1875-1911.

———. Purdue Registry of Officers and Alumni. The Virginia Kelly Karnes Archives and Special Collections Research Center, Purdue University Libraries. West Lafayette, IN, 1865-1915.

Great Britain marriage record, 1827. Accessed October 31, 2013. *Ancestry.com*.

Guide to the Chicago Manual Training Records, 1882-1913. Special Collections Research Center, University of Chicago Library.

Leah Rowena Miller Scrapbook. The Virginia Kelly Karnes Archives and Special Collections Research Center, Purdue University Libraries.

Marcus, J. "A Note from Kansas." *Exponent* (West Lafayette, IN), Sept. 16, 1903.

Mayer, H., and R. Wade. *Chicago Growth of a Metropolis*. Chicago: University of Chicago Press, 1969.

Pacyga, D. *Chicago: A Biography*. Chicago: University of Chicago Press, 2009.

Purdue Alumni Directory. The Virginia Kelly Karnes Archives and Special Collections Research Center, Purdue University Libraries. West Lafayette, IN, 1875-1906.

———. The Virginia Kelly Karnes Archives and Special Collections Research Center, Purdue University Libraries. West Lafayette, IN, 1875-1934.

Purdue *Debris*. 1904. The Virginia Kelly Karnes Archives and Special Collections Research Center, Purdue University Libraries.

Shortridge, James. *The Middle West: Its Meaning in American Culture*. Lawrence: University Press of Kansas, 1989.

Spears, T. *Chicago Dreaming: Midwesterners and the City, 1871-1919*. Chicago: University of Chicago Press, 2005.

United States Federal Censuses, 1890 to 1910. Accessed October 31, 2013. *Ancestry.com*.

United States Federal Census, 1930. William R. Davis, Douglas, AZ. Accessed October 19, 2013. *Ancestry.com*.

Williams, Raymond. *The Country and the City*. New York: Oxford University Press, 1973.

Notes

1. Information about Davis's former institution provided from *Debris*, 1904, the Virginia Kelly Karnes Archives and Special Collections Research Center, Purdue University Libraries.

2. Timothy Spears, *Chicago Dreaming: Midwesterners and the City, 1871-1919* (Chicago: University of Chicago Press, 2005).

3. United States Federal Census, 1920, accessed October 31, 2013, *Ancestry.com*.

4. Spears, *Chicago Dreaming*, 181.

5. Dominic Pacyga, *Chicago: A Biography* (Chicago: University of Chicago Press, 2009), 33. According to Pacyga, "Despite the call of Know Nothings, a nativist political movement that spread across the United States, including Chicago in the 1850s, and others for an end to immigration, the city depended on the foreigners who had settled within its borders."

6. Harold Mayer and Richard White, *Chicago: Growth of a Metropolis* (Chicago: University of Chicago Press, 1969), 64.

7. *Debris*, 1904.

8. Great Britain marriage record, 1827, accessed October 31, 2013, *Ancestry.com*. Information obtained through the process of elimination through *Ancestry.com*.

9. United States Federal Censuses, 1890-1910, accessed October 31, 2013, *Ancestry.com*.

10. According to the University of Chicago archival records, it was an academic and vocational institute for young men of high school age to explore the technical field of engineering. In the year 1903, the Training School became a part of the University of Chicago Laboratory Schools. Guide to the Chicago Manual Training Records. Special Collections Research Center, University of Chicago Library, 1882-1913.

11. Daniel Lichter and David Brown, "Rural America in an Urban Society: Changing Spatial and Social Boundaries," *Annual Review of Sociology* 566, no. 37 (2011).

12. J. Clyde Marcus, "A Note from Kansas," *Exponent* (West Lafayette, IN), Sept. 16, 1903.

13. Spears, *Chicago Dreaming*, 77.

14. *Debris*, 1904.

15. This is an excerpt from a poem in the 1904 *Debris* regarding the class of 1904: "At the dime museum on Fifth Street the barker was expatiating on the wonderful characteristics of the devilfish.

'The devilfish has ten mouths,' he bawled, and pointing to Farkas, continued, 'But he doesn't make half as much noise with all ten of 'em as our fuzzy friend yonder does with his one.'" Ibid., 15.

16. *Debris*, 1904.

17. Ibid., 15. Purdue University students experienced a tragic train crash on the way to the Indiana University versus Purdue football game in Indianapolis. The crash involved train cars carrying Purdue faculty, students, the football team, and band.

18. *Debris*, 1904.

19. Spears, *Chicago Dreaming*, 20.

20. Due to Emil's hard work and forging his way for a better life, one of his sons was able to become a musician. United States Federal Census, 1940, accessed October, 19, 2013, *Ancestry.com*.

21. United States Federal Census Bureau, 1930.

22. The Purdue Alumni Directory is a self-reporting directory of Purdue alumni.

23. Purdue Alumni Directory, the Virginia Kelly Karnes Archives and Special Collections Research Center, Purdue University Libraries, West Lafayette, IN, 1875-1934.

24. As illustrated in Leah R. Miller's 1920s scrapbook, Chicago was still a place of wonder and exploration. Leah and her friends visited the city of Chicago for a home economics inspection trip during the 1920s. She illustrated her trip in her scrapbook with clippings of Chicago landmarks and even the letterhead from the hotel where she stayed.

Joseph Burke Knapp: "A Barnacle on the Ship of Progress"

Alexandria Nickolas

Almost all of us face challenging times. Whether it is losing a loved one, being involved in a war, or going bankrupt, the unifying factor that defines us is how we rise from these tragedies. It seems that there are so many stories of people giving up when times get rough, and not enough about someone who rose above to triumph over the troubling times. Joseph Knapp did just that. While Joe might have seemed like a normal family man and businessperson, his life was filled with tragedies that would have stopped many people from moving on. The defining characteristic of this man was his drive for success. His family remembers him as a man who would never say no, who stayed true to his word, and who would fight for what he wanted. He never let tragedies stop him from becoming the successful man he knew he wanted to be. This is Joseph Knapp's story, his rise from tragedy to triumph.

Joseph Burke Knapp was born on October 3, 1880, in Evansville, Indiana, to Mary and Dr. Emil Knapp.[1] His father was a well-known dental surgeon of the town and was credited with taking graduate courses each year to stay in tune with the evolving profession.[2] Joe went on to attend the local high school and made quite a name for himself in athletics.[3] He was even the captain of his high school's football team.[4]

He started a promising career at Purdue in 1900. With a nickname of "Joeie" and an "Evansville *Morning Courier* in his hand," he spent his freshman year acquiring many friends, all the while being known for his shy nature.[5] He soon joined the Sigma Nu fraternity, the class baseball team, the football team, the basketball team, and the athletic association, of which he was vice president during his freshman year. While Joe was an outstanding student, what really made him a cut above was his involvement in athletics, and his scrapbook from his years at Purdue records his athletic achievement in detail. This old but sturdy scrapbook compiled during his college years is stuffed with numerous articles about his athletic games and Purdue's victories. Articles about Purdue's basketball team state that Joe earned the title of team captain during his freshman year.[6] He and his team even went on to win the national championship in 1901.[7] Joe was also very prominent in football at Purdue. He was known as being "fast on his feet" and was a very good halfback.[8] Through his time at Purdue, he helped his team win many games in both football and basketball.[9] His love for athletics was prominent in his activities and everyday life. Unfortunately, at the start of his senior year he hurt his knee and was not allowed to play football.[10] Though he did not know it at the time, his ability to play athletics would soon end for the rest of his life.

On October 31, 1903, Joe boarded a train with his football team and many other students on their way to an exciting game against Indiana University. As the train was arriving in Indianapolis, something went terribly wrong and the train collided head-on with a freight engine. Joe was in the head car along with his teammates, and they went straight into the collision. Throughout the entire wreck, he never lost consciousness. He recalled that when the front end of the car gave way, he instantly grasped the severity of the situation and braced himself for impact, folding his arms and placing them around his knees. He was thrown from the car, hit the ground, and rolled until he landed in a ditch. He was dazed and confused, but was soon carried to a doctor for treatment. His right knee was badly injured, the same knee that was already hurt before the accident. The bones in his knee had been "forced apart," his ligaments torn, and shin bone broken. In an article pasted in his scrapbook, Joe told a reporter that he was hopeful that he would soon be able to walk on crutches, but had not fully recovered mentally from the terrible accident.[11] He said that "the sound of the terrible crash" rang in his ears, and we can imagine the sorrow he felt at losing so many teammates and friends.[12] A total of seventeen lives were lost in the wreck, fourteen of whom were Purdue football players.[13] He stayed at his family's home in Evansville while he recovered. An article describing Joe's recovery mentions that his family was overjoyed that their son was safe and not badly injured. While recovering, he received numerous letters from friends, family, and his fraternity.[14]

He returned to Purdue in January of 1904,[15] but sadly he was not able to return to Purdue athletics.[16] Though the train wreck was a major setback both academically and emotionally, he did not let it stop him from graduating in June 1904 with a degree in civil engineering. His speedy recovery from the train wreck seemed to be a defining moment for the character of Joe himself; even though he had endured a great tragedy, he made the best of it and kept going on with his life, never losing his drive for success.

After graduation, he went to work for the Department of Agriculture in the Division of Forestry. Though the jump from civil engineering to forestry seems confusing, Joe used his knowledge of engineering to help pioneer a new technology involving wood and the transportation of food. Joe's studies from Purdue helped him think creatively, and he pursued a career outside of his civil engineering degree. In the early 1900s, professionals trained in forestry were very scarce in the United States. While forestry was popular in other parts of the world, the United States did not have a forestry department until 1876, and the department's main concern in its early years was the preservation of forests.[17] Historian Harold T. Pinkett explains that the US Forest Service progressed in 1905 when control over federal forests was handed to the Department of Agriculture, which had a "growing staff of foresters" who truly had knowledge about forests.[18] Along with the adjustment of control in the department came a great expansion of federal forests, and in return more room for testing and preservation of precious trees and timber. This expansion was even supported by Theodore Roosevelt in a White House conference in 1908.[19]

This expansion of the department could not have come at a better time for Joe. Critical tests were being performed throughout the nation, including at Purdue, on the strength and manufacturing properties of wood.[20] Joe's expertise on the durability of different woods is shown through his government publications, such as *Fire Killed Douglas Fir*, in which he explains the properties of deterioration rates of Douglas fir trees and the length of time fire-killed timber remains marketable.[21] Another publication by Joe and McGarvey Cline is entitled *Properties and Uses of Douglas Fir*. It contains two parts that explain the mechanical properties of Douglas fir and also the commercial uses of the timber.[22] In 1913 Joe wrote an article, "Reasons Why Government Should Not Compete in Manufacture of Lumber," for the December 1 issue of the *West Coast Lumberman*. At this time, the United States government was arguing that ownership of timber should not be concentrated in the hands of a few private owners in fear that they would form a de facto monopoly. Joe was clearly on the side of private businesses, arguing that a "certain concentration of ownership is essential." In his article, he explains that lumber had contributed more to the economic wealth of the nation, at that time, than any other industry. Through this article, and his government publications, we can see not only the passion he had for his profession, but also his political and economic interests in forestry.

While Joe was starting his career, he married Cornelia Pinkham in 1911 and soon had two sons, Joseph Burke, Jr. and Robert.[23] Not long after, however, tragedy struck once again. In 1916, Cornelia became ill with tuberculosis. She was sent to California in hopes of recovering, but her health took a turn for the worse after a month in treatment. Joe was notified immediately of her deteriorating condition and left Portland to be by her side in California. Unfortunately, he did not make it in time, for she died before he was able to comfort her.[24] Through this truly tragic time in which other people might give up and mourn, Joe did not stop his fast-paced life. His children were sent to live with Cornelia's family while he moved to Bend, Oregon, to work for the Shevlin-Hixon Company. While it may seem Joe abandoned his children for his job so soon after their mother's death, this was not the case. Joe was a very hardworking man who always wanted to provide and do what was best for his children. His departure and eventual reunion with his children should be seen as a testament for his desire to be a "family man," for he always wanted to provide for his children.

While in the Shevlin-Hixon Company, Joe researched the manufacture of box shook, a new technology that became very important for the transportation of food.[25] In the early nineteenth century, food was mainly packaged and distributed through tin cans.[26] Joe helped take manufacturing crates for food distribution to the next level. With the new development of box shook, food crates were manufactured with small holes in them that allowed for proper ventilation of the food the crates were carrying. These small holes were made possible by interweaving the wooden slats of the crates. This allowed food to be transported for longer distances, because the interweaving of the wood kept rodents out and ensured that the food would not rot.[27] During the time that box shook technology was being produced, World War I began. Joe fought the battle at home and was deeply involved with the efforts of the US Food Administration, which was tasked with the manufacturing and

FIGURE 1. JOE KNAPP. COURTESY OF HIATT KNAPP.

processing of wood packaging, something that was vital to the US troops for the shipment of fresh food and other supplies.[28] Joe's effort in introducing the new box shook technology and its use for the production of crates and the transportation of food could have been the most important part of our success in the war. If it were not for Joe and the US Food Administration's expertise and knowledge of box shook technology, fresh food might not have been successfully transported to our troops and they, in turn, could have starved. It is at this point in his life that we again see Joe's astonishing ability to turn tragic events into progressive action. He seemed to never back down or say no to a fight. Along with many other men across the nation, whether fighting in the war or helping the war efforts at home, he worked as hard as he could to help the country in need.

After the success of the manufacturing of box shook crates for World War I, Joe utilized his extensive knowledge about the strength and durability of wood to create his own company, the Joseph B. Knapp Company, in 1920. The company was based in Portland, Oregon, and he was able to have his children back with him. The same year, he married Helene Dalrymple, who gave birth to a daughter, Mary Caroline, in 1921. Joe's life seemed to be full again. With a strong family and children by his side, it seemed that nothing could go wrong. His company sold to a variety of people in a range of places. Its distribution of boxes spread from fruit growers and packers here in America, all the way to Germany, Belgium, and the United Kingdom.[29]

Unfortunately, tragedy struck not only Joe's life, but that of many other Americans as well in 1929. The Great Depression took quite a toll on Joe's company, driving him into bankruptcy. He was forced to sell his elegant house in Portland and move into a very small apartment. Joe had to borrow money from people to stay afloat during this tough time.[30] Perhaps the most telling thing about his attitude is what he did after the Depression, when he was back on his feet financially. He took trains from Portland and sought out the people he had borrowed money from to pay them back fully in cash. Even if the people had passed away, he gave the money to their families.[31] Joe would never let tragedy or hard times stop him from keeping his word, and his pursuit to pay back those who helped him in a time of need shows this aspect of his personality.

While Joe survived tragedy after tragedy in his life, he never stopped fighting for his success. He would always rise up to the challenge in front of him, and in the midst of World War II, he did just that for yet another time in his life. During World War II, Joe fought on the home front again on the logistical side of the fight. His job was to calculate the proper quantities of wood for the manufacture of box shook crates, arrange for saw mills to cut the trees to the proper size, and then arrange for the wood grain to be sent to the right places at the right time all around the West Coast. Joe's company achieved national recognition during World War II for his work with the army and navy by supplying ammunition containers and lumber supplies for military trucks.[32] Though he did not receive any awards for his tremendous efforts to aid the war, Joe gained a deep personal satisfaction for his work. It was yet again that he rose to greatness during tragic times.[33] Joe's very successful life came to an end soon after the war. Purdue's graduating class of 1904 celebrated their fiftieth anniversary in 1954, and though he was too sick to attend, the class paid him tribute by telephoning him on a loud speaker for all to hear so he could still feel the love of his past classmates and Purdue.[34]

FIGURE 2. JOE KNAPP.
COURTESY OF HIATT KNAPP.

On July 9, 1954, Joseph Knapp's life came to an end after battling with a year-long illness.

Looking back on Joe's life, it seemed that with every tragedy he faced he came out stronger in the end. From his wife passing away, to going bankrupt, to enduring not just one but two world wars, he would not withdraw from the fight. It is easy to see his work ethic through times such as World War I and II, when he helped create a food packaging technology that allowed for US troops to be fed. Through this light, we can look at him as a hero, as someone who always kept his word, and fought to make his life a successful one while remaining humble. As remembered by his grandson, Joe's stock line when receiving a compliment was, "I'm just a barnacle on the ship of progress."[35] From Joseph's Knapp's tragedies and triumphs, anyone can learn that no matter what you face, if you work hard you can always rise to the top.

Bibliography

Arieli, Melosy Amsel. "Tin Cans." *History Magazine* 12, no. 5 (2011): 6–7.

"Joseph Knapp Dies at 74 After Career in Lumber." *The Oregonian*. July 10, 1954.

Knapp, Joseph. Scrapbook. Personal collection of Mickey Knapp in Portland, Oregon.

Knapp, Louis. Interview by Alexandria Nickolas. E-mail. November 7, 2013.

———. Interview by Alexandria Nickolas. Phone. November 14, 2013.

Lockert, Andrew. Interview by Alexandria Nickolas. Phone. November 16, 2013.

Lockley, Fred. *History of the Columbia River Valley, from the Dalles to the Sea*. Vol. 2. S. J. Clarke Publishing, 1928.

Exponent (West Lafayette, IN), Jan. 7, 1904.

Purdue *Debris*. 1904. The Virginia Kelly Karnes Archives and Special Collections Research Center, Purdue University Libraries.

Notes

1. Fred Lockley, *History of the Columbia River Valley, from the Dalles to the Sea* (S. J. Clarke Publishing, 1928), 699.

2. Ibid., 699.

3. Ibid., 699.

4. Joseph Knapp, scrapbook, personal collection of Mickey Knapp in Portland, Oregon, 39.

5. *Debris*, 1904, the Virginia Kelly Karnes Archives and Special Collections Research Center, Purdue University Libraries, 91.

6. Personal scrapbook of Joseph Knapp, 38.

7. Ibid., article, "Purdue's Champions at Basketball," 27.

8. Ibid., 9.

9. Ibid., article, "Purdue Basketball Team," 21.

10. Ibid., article, "Purdue Working Hard," 64.

11. Ibid., article, "Knapp Comes Home Almost Recovered," 47.

12. Ibid., 47.

13. "The Disaster," *Exponent* (West Lafayette, IN), Nov. 11, 1903, 1.

14. Ibid., 52–57

15. *Exponent*, Jan. 7, 1904.

16. Louis Knapp (grandson of Joseph Knapp), interview by Alexandria Nickolas, phone, November 14, 2013.

17. On the development of forestry in America, see: Harold T. Pinkett, "Forestry Comes to America," *Agricultural History* 54, no. 1 (Jan. 1980): 4–10.

18. Ibid., 9.

19. Ibid., 4-10.

20. Page 5 of the September 23, 1903 *Exponent* writes about Timber Testing stations that were being added to Purdue.

21. US Department of Agriculture, *Fire Killed Douglas Fir: A Study of Deterioration, Usability and Strength,* by Joseph Burke Knapp, Washington: Government Printing Office, 1912 (US Department of Agriculture, Forestry Division Bulletin no. 112).

22. US Department of Agriculture, *Properties and Uses of Douglas Fir,* by Joseph Burke Knapp and McGarvey Cline, Washington: Government Printing Office, 1911 (US Department of Agriculture, Forestry Division Bulletin no. 88).

23. Lockley, "History of the Columbia River Valley," 699.

24. Article, "Local Woman Dies at Sierra Madre, Near Los Angeles," 1916, personally owned by Rosalind Knapp, Washington, DC.

25. Lockley, "History of the Columbia River Valley," 699.

26. Melosy Amsel Arieli, "Tin Cans," *History Magazine* 12, no. 5 (2011): 6-7.

27. Louis Knapp (grandson of Joseph Knapp), interview by Alexandria Nickolas, e-mail, November 7, 2013.

28. Ibid.

29. Lockley, "History of the Columbia River Valley," 699.

30. Andrew Lockert (grandson of Joseph Knapp), interview by Alexandria Nickolas, phone, November 16, 2013.

31. Louis Knapp (grandson of Joseph Knapp), interview by Alexandria Nickolas, phone, November 14, 2013.

32. "Joseph Knapp Dies at 74 After Career in Lumber," *The Oregonian,* July 10, 1954.

33. Andrew Lockert (grandson of Joseph Knapp), interview by Alexandria Nickolas, phone, November 16, 2013.

34. "Joseph Knapp Dies at 74 After Career in Lumber," *The Oregonian,* July 10, 1954.

35. Andrew Lockert (grandson of Joseph Knapp), interview by Alexandria Nickolas, phone, November 16, 2013.

Fitting In but Sticking Out: The Life of an Immigrant Student at Purdue in 1904

Lindy Schubring

Young people growing up in early twentieth-century America experienced exhilarating and trying times as the country developed economically, culturally, and socially. They lived through the second Industrial Revolution, two world wars, the Roaring Twenties, and the Great Depression. Important social change swept through America, which brought new inventions, new ideals, and new societal norms.

People in Indiana were not exempt from the changes occurring in the United States. In fact, they experienced much of this change firsthand. The Morrill Act of 1862 funded new land-grant universities, which gave farmers and working-class people the option of receiving higher education in mechanics and agriculture. A more educated populous shaped the culture of not only Indiana, but also the rest of the country.

The idea of attending college daunts, yet excites, new students. As a college student myself, I understand the major transition that happens when one first moves away from home to go to college. It can be a challenge to find a niche in the larger university community, but once a student does so, he or she will create fond memories that will last a lifetime. Unfortunately, not everyone has a positive college experience and may desire to disconnect himself or herself from the university after graduation. One student from the Purdue University class of 1904 suffered such a fate. Hugo Alex Berthold lost contact with Purdue after graduation, suggesting that he did not have an enjoyable experience. He may not have relished his studies or extracurricular involvement; he may have had a prickly personality; or he may not have felt particularly nostalgic. Although we can never know for certain, evidence from the Virginia Kelly Karnes Archives and Special Collections Research Center as well as Purdue publications suggests that Hugo's immigrant status may have been the key factor that set him apart from his peers.

Hugo migrated with his family from Germany and settled in New York City. Despite being an immigrant, the editors of the *Debris,* Purdue's yearbook, described him as being "as thorough an American as any of us who have never been outside the limits of our own chicken yard."[1] The fact that Hugo's peers considered an immigrant like him an American may not seem significant to us today, but it was a high compliment in the early 1900s.

As a member of Purdue's class of 1904, Hugo studied electrical engineering. He had a large presence on campus, immersing himself in a variety of student clubs and organizations, in most of which he held leadership positions.[2] Hugo belonged to many student committees, including the 1904 Banquet Committee, the Military Ball Committee, and the Senior Banquet Committee. Hugo also seemed to enjoy writing. He actively participated in the Irving Literary Society for four years and worked as a reporter for the school newspaper, the *Exponent*. He handled money and finances as the treasurer of the Irving Literary Society his second year, as the class treasurer his latter two years, and as the advertising manager for the *Debris*. In addition, Hugo belonged to the Purdue branch of the American Institute of Electrical Engineers, the Minuet Club, and the Athletic Association.[3] He also served as a cadet captain. Hugo partook in a wide variety of student organizations, and he served the campus community continuously.

From the outside, Hugo appeared to have an enjoyable experience at Purdue. The unfortunate and perplexing aspect of Hugo's life is that he lost contact with the University after graduation. He did not attend class reunions and did not share information about his employment status. According to the Purdue alumni magazine, the *Alumnus*, thirty-one of his peers attended "Alumni Day" in March 1915, and as of June 1915, eighty-one of his peers subscribed to the magazine. Included in these lists are many students who belonged to the same organizations as Hugo and demonstrated a similar level of involvement within the student body. However, Hugo himself neither attended Alumni Day nor was included in the list of magazine subscribers.[4] Despite his involvement on campus as a student, Hugo's immersion in University activities did not extend to his postgraduate life. The source of his ultimate disconnection could be rooted in his involvement in clubs, ethnic discrimination, or interactions with other students.

During Hugo's senior year, the *Exponent* published a letter in which an alumnus wrote to his younger brother, giving him advice about how to best spend his time at Purdue. The alumnus recommended that his younger brother "go into college enterprises and do things outside [his] school work, not with the idea of getting honors, but for the mere pleasure of accomplishing something worthwhile."[5] A possible reason for Hugo's detachment is that he was involved in too many activities at once, perhaps for honors, rather than interest. As a foreigner, Hugo probably tried his best to fit into the student body at Purdue and find his niche in the community. However, being involved in multiple clubs at once could have been overwhelming and counterproductive, leading to weaker connections with his peers, and ultimately making him feel excluded from the student body.

Another, perhaps more obvious, reason for Hugo's disconnection could be that he did not have many friends at Purdue. Although cultural stereotypes may have affected Hugo greatly, the answer for his disappearance could simply lie in the fact that no one really liked him. Hugo was bold and outspoken, and these qualities may have deterred relationships with his classmates. The *Debris* described Hugo as "the champion leg puller" of the school. His persistence and boldness guaranteed he would get his way. The *Debris* includes an account of Hugo "wheedling the Commandant" into letting the students use the armory for the annual

Mechanics Burning.[6] Hugo also was notorious for his temper. A line in a poem in the *Debris* reads: "What would you think / If you saw . . . / Berthold calm and possessed?"[7] A report in the Irving Literary Society daily journal on May 20, 1904, documents an instance when the leaders of the society disciplined Hugo during a meeting. Two of the members, Mr. Grant and Mr. Herrick, were fined 25 cents (about $6.58 today) for speaking during the extemporaneous speeches. Hugo, enraged by the injustice of this motion against his peers, was fined 5 cents for "misconduct during the discussion of this motion."[8] Furthermore, a fictional story titled "A Wheel from the Head of a Famous '04" illustrates Hugo's aggression by describing a time when Hugo met with a *Debris* reporter to tell him of his breakthrough invention. Hugo had the great idea for something he called "Antisalt." If people found their food to be too salty, they could sprinkle Antisalt on it to negate the saltiness. Hugo argued his invention was critical for newlywed couples, where the wife was still learning how to cook properly. The most curious part of this story is the way in which Hugo told the *Debris* reporter about his idea. He forcefully pins the reporter against a wall to make him understand the importance of his invention.[9] Although this story was fictional, it illustrates how Hugo's peers viewed him as aggressive and found it entertaining to portray him in such a way.

No matter how American Hugo's peers viewed him to be, he was always remembered as an immigrant. There is an account in the *Debris* of Hugo using the word "stenographer" in place of the word "typewriter" during a meeting.[10] It is possible that Hugo thought he was using the correct word to describe the physical typewriter, but accidentally confused it with the word describing the person who takes notes. Although misusing an English word was a simple mistake, Hugo's peers found it humorous nonetheless. Hugo's foreign roots made him an object of ridicule for his classmates, not necessarily because they wanted to be cruel, but rather, they found the cultural differences between themselves and their German classmate entertaining. Although their intentions were likely harmless, their words may have ended up really hurting Hugo.

Another possible explanation for Hugo's sudden disappearance is that he faced outright hostility from his fellow students and faculty because of his German roots. Feelings of unrest and resentment surged through America in the twentieth century, and with that came anti-German sentiments. These feelings infiltrated the culture through mass media, entertainment, and social interaction. Specifically, theater and public entertainment circulated cultural beliefs.

Popular theater includes vaudeville, burlesque, musical entertainment, circus, and minstrelsy. Compared to legitimate theater shows, which detailed grandiose tales of noble kings leading large armies into glorious battles, popular theater shows portrayed everyday tasks and relationships. At the turn of the century, serious playwriting shifted from melodrama to realism, which was "more vigorous, varied, and competent than ever before."[11] Realism, as the name suggests, reflects everyday life, and it is a more approachable and relatable version of theater. Realistic plays were "rooted deeply in the polyglot character of America," and thereby appealed to many people, including foreigners and infrequent theatergoers.[12] The United States saw exponential growth in the number of immigrants from the mid- to late 1800s, and this rapid growth increased the audience of theater shows.

Minstrel shows, although notoriously offensive in content, played an important part in American culture because they "provided their audiences with one of the only bases that many of them had for understanding America's increasing ethnic diversity."[13] The performances influenced the American people's understanding of different cultures, but they often did so in an untruthful, exaggerated way. Minstrel performances typically are understood to mean only blackface acting, but their repertoire expanded beyond that. Minstrels also gave performances ridiculing European and Asian immigrants. Because of the entertaining nature of the shows, they exaggerated the immigrants' peculiar features and downplayed or ignored presumably more "American" ones. Consequently, they embedded stereotypes into their audiences' minds.

As theater historian Robert C. Toll notes, out of all the immigrants, minstrels treated Germans the most kindly. They portrayed Germans as hardworking, practical people, whose only faults were that they drank too much lager and ate too much sauerkraut and sausage. Despite their "hefty physiques and even heftier appetites," minstrels represented Germans as being very courteous, almost enough to be an example for American citizens.[14] In fact, "Germans fit so well into white American values and world-view that they served as model immigrants."[15] They gained respect from their fellow Americans because "they earned themselves a place . . . by fighting valiantly for the Union."[16] Therefore, the minstrels portrayed Germans as positively as they could while still making their performances entertaining.[17] The fact that Germans were white-skinned also made them more easily acceptable than African Americans or Asians, for example. Nevertheless, Germans on stage were still treated stereotypically.

Moreover, the fact that Germans received relatively fair treatment on the stage did not free them from hostility in the real world. The anxiety building up to World War I sparked anti-German sentiments throughout the country. Americans forced Germans to change the names of their businesses, change their own names, and to speak English, rather than German, in public areas. This harsh treatment continued until the United States declared war on Germany in 1917, when the flame of anti-German attitudes blazed into a raging fire. Many German shops closed, and concert programs and weddings no longer played German music. Furthermore, "Americans who spoke German were threatened with violence or boycotts."[18] Even though minstrels specifically did not paint Germans in a very harsh light, that did not mean the rest of society followed their lead in the early part of the twentieth century.

Noncommercial theaters became popular on college campuses in the 1920s. Purdue had its own active minstrel society, the Purdue Thermo Minstrels. They performed a couple of times throughout the school year, and their performances would often benefit the Athletic Association. The 1904 *Debris* contains a program of the Thermo Minstrels' performances.[19] Most notably, the Olio, or miscellaneous collection, included a piece titled "German Comedians." It is safe to assume this show would seem offensive to us today, and the hostility may have been extreme enough to encourage Hugo to disconnect himself from Purdue in 1904. If "German Comedians" documented Germans similarly to other American minstrel shows, Hugo may or may not have felt offended by the content in the show. However, that does not mean that Hugo did not feel resentment from his peers on a daily basis. We cannot accurately judge the severity of anti-German sentiment on Purdue's campus, but it could have been cruel enough to foster Hugo's disconnection.

Evidence from the Purdue *Alumni Directory* suggests that Hugo lived a fulfilling life after graduation. Hugo resided on a small farm near Calgary, Alberta, for two years. He rented the farm out before moving to New York City to work as an assistant manager of Duhrssen and Pfaltz, an electrical company operated by first-generation Germans.[20] Because Hugo was included among the "lost graduates," the information about his employment was provided secondhand.[21] Even though Hugo found a stable job after graduation, he did not share his successes with the University.

From the outside, Hugo seemed to fare well both as a student at Purdue and after graduation. However, Hugo did not invest as much in the University upon graduation as did most of his peers. A possible explanation for his lack of involvement is that Hugo did not have an enjoyable experience at Purdue, and thus, he desired to disassociate himself with the University. A variety of factors could have encouraged his ultimate disconnection: being involved in too many extracurriculars at once, a poor relationship with his peers, and ethnic discrimination on campus. Another possible but entirely different explanation could be that Hugo became very busy after graduation and simply did not have the time or resources to attend class reunions or donate money to the University. The unfortunate aspect of Hugo's life lies in the fact that a seemingly successful and happy individual desired to distance himself from his alma mater. Hugo seemed to fit well into student life at Purdue, but because of his German roots, he stood apart from the rest of his peers. This isolation could have been severe enough to cause Hugo to separate himself from the University. Even if he was not happy while he attended Purdue University, I can only hope that Hugo found happiness in the rest of his life.

Bibliography

Irving Literary Society Papers 1875–1925. The Virginia Kelly Karnes Archives and Special Collections Research Center, Purdue University Libraries.

Jack. "A Letter of Advice." *Exponent* (West Lafayette, IN), Dec. 9, 1903.

Purdue *Alumni Bulletin*. April 1909–June 1915. The Virginia Kelly Karnes Archives and Special Collections Research Center, Purdue University Libraries.

"Purdue Alumni Directory 1875–1934." The Virginia Kelly Karnes Archives and Special Collections Research Center, Purdue University Libraries.

Purdue *Alumni Magazine* 1914–1915. The Virginia Kelly Karnes Archives and Special Collections Research Center, Purdue University Libraries.

Purdue *Debris*. 1904. The Virginia Kelly Karnes Archives and Special Collections Research Center, Purdue University Libraries.

Telegram on October 31, 1903, Series 1, Box 13-14, Winthrop E. Stone Papers, 1870s-1920s. The Virginia Kelly Karnes Archives and Special Collections Research Center, Purdue University Libraries.

Toll, Robert C. *Blacking Up: The Minstrel Show in Nineteenth-Century America*. New York: Oxford University Press, 1974.

Twain, Mark. "The Awful German Language." In *The Comic Mark Twain Reader*, edited by Charles Neider, 277–92. New York: Doubleday & Company, Inc., 1977.

"Shadows of War." *Library of Congress*. Accessed November 30, 2013. http://www.loc.gov/teachers/classroommaterials/presentationsandactivities/presentations/immigration/german8.html.

Wilson, Garff B. *Three Hundred Years of American Drama and Theatre: From Ye Bare and Ye Cubb to Chorus Line*. Englewood Cliffs, NJ: Prentice-Hall, 1982.

Notes

1. *Debris*, 1904, the Virginia Kelly Karnes Archives and Special Collections Research Center, Purdue University Libraries.

2. Ibid., 69.

3. Most members of the Athletic Association were on the train that suffered the terrible accident on October 31, 1903. There is a heart-wrenching telegram from Hugo's father desperately asking President Stone whether or not his son was on the train. Hugo was not listed among the injured, but it is unknown whether or not he was on board at the time of the accident. Telegram on October 31, 1903, Series 1, Box 13-14, Winthrop E. Stone Papers, 1870s-1920s, the Virginia Kelly Karnes Archives and Special Collections Research Center, Purdue University Libraries.

4. Purdue *Alumni Bulletin*, April 1909–June 1915, the Virginia Kelly Karnes Archives and Special Collections Research Center, Purdue University Libraries.

5. Jack, "A Letter of Advice," *Exponent* (West Lafayette, IN), Dec. 9, 1903.

6. Ibid., 276. The annual Mechanics Burning was a student ritual in which the seniors performed a mock funeral ceremony and burned an effigy of the author of their hydraulics textbook.

7. Ibid., 300.

8. Irving Literary Society Papers 1875-1925, the Virginia Kelly Karnes Archives and Special Collections Research Center, Purdue University Libraries.

9. *Debris*, 1904, 263.

10. Ibid., 301.

11. Garff B. Wilson, *Three Hundred Years of American Drama and Theatre: From Ye Bare and Ye Cubb to Chorus Line* (Englewood Cliffs, NJ: Prentice-Hall, 1982).

12. Ibid., 122.

13. Robert C. Toll, *Blacking Up: The Minstrel Show in Nineteenth-Century America* (New York: Oxford University Press, 1974).

14. Ibid., 173.

15. Ibid., 175.

16. Ibid., 174.

17. Minstrels mainly mocked the obscurity of German language in their shows. Other media, including texts like "The Awful German Language," a short story by Mark Twain, mocked the language as well. In this story, Twain points out the flaws in the German language in a humorous but not overly disrespectful way.

18. "Shadows of War," *Library of Congress*, accessed November 30, 2013, http://www.loc.gov/teachers/classroommaterials/presentationsandactivities/presentations/immigration/german8.html.

19. *Debris,* 1904, 184–85.

20. "Purdue Alumni Directory 1875–1934," the Virginia Kelly Karnes Archives and Special Collections Research Center, Purdue University.

21. Purdue *Alumni Magazine* 1914–1915, the Virginia Kelly Karnes Archives and Special Collections Research Center, Purdue University Libraries.

Far from Home and Far from Normal: The Experience of an International Student on an American College Campus at the Turn of the Twentieth Century

Vivian Gu

Listed under the "Seniors" section of Purdue University's 1904 *Debris*, there is a Japanese study-abroad student by the name of Sukichi Yoshisaka.[1] He is the only Asian senior to be found in the *Debris* that year. On a campus that was thoroughly dominated by white students at the time, during a period in American history when the rising population of immigrants was making people across the nation question just what it meant to be "American," one might wonder how a student like Sukichi was treated by his peers. By studying cases such as that of Sukichi, we can determine how the student body perceived the presence of international students and the type of experience such a student had in an American college setting at the turn of the twentieth century.

During the school year of 1903–1904, there was a significant interest at Purdue in foreign cultures. One particularly striking instance of that interest is in the number of fictional stories that featured some aspects from other cultures and nations and portrayed them in peculiar ways, which were published in the 1903–1904 editions of the University's newspaper, the *Exponent*. For example, a featured story from the September 16, 1903 edition of the paper, titled "The Egyptian Vases," told a fictional account of an Egyptian student on Purdue's campus and discussed spiritual phenomena involving an ornate vase and the pursuit of crown jewels.[2] Another example includes a story in the September 23, 1903 edition, called "Mister Kinnigan Tells of His 'Soonday Axkurshun'," which poked fun at the Scottish accent.[3] While the purpose of these two stories seemed to be to exploit the "strangeness" of other cultures for the reader's entertainment, not all such stories were necessarily meant to make fun of any particular society. This presence of foreign cultures in *Exponent* stories shows that, regardless of whether the views on foreign cultures were positive or negative, the majority of students had an overall fascination with them at the time. Furthermore, another example from the September 23 edition of the *Exponent* is a section entitled "A Letter from Professor Robertson," which discussed how some white missionaries wished to become more involved with the Chinese.[4] This particular account was chronicled in the *Exponent* editions throughout the rest of the school year, and it showcased an intent to convert those from other cultures to become what Americans at the time considered more "enlightened."

Some of the apparent interest in other cultures on campus during the 1903–1904 year also can be seen in how members of the senior class interacted with the international students. Besides Sukichi Yoshisaka, there were other study-abroad seniors listed in the 1904 *Debris* who serve as examples of how foreign students were treated during this time on Purdue's campus. While there were many students who identified as "foreign," due to having been born outside of the United States, I intend to focus on the students who were studying abroad rather than those who had immigrated. Two such students, Milan Karchoff from Bulgaria and Alex Lindsay from Great Britain, were often associated with Sukichi within the text of the *Debris*. Milan's biographical description claims that he desires an American wife and insists that he has a "princely bearing."[5] Alex's description states that, "His noble and polished brow shining for the want of nature's covering soon turned all fear of military harm into wonder at the intellectual foreigner,"[6] in which the editors of the *Debris* imply that Alex had an intelligent and no-nonsense or perhaps even imposing air about him, which his peers associated with his heritage. Sukichi, Alex, and Milan were all listed together under Alex's description with the label of "the beloved foreigners."[7] While these statements could be seen as lighthearted and joking in nature, and many other students were subjected to mockery of their character in the *Debris*, the writers seem to have been specifically mocking the fact that these three were not from the United States. Historian Whitney Walton argues in *Internationalism, National Identities, and Study Abroad: France and the United States, 1890–1970* that the word "foreign" holds a connotation of being inherently different or strange in some manner.[8] The editors of the *Debris* grouped the international students together despite the three being of very different backgrounds and temperaments, and one can construe that the student body was, in a way, isolating the international students and labeling them as "the others."

Also worth mentioning is that in Sukichi's depiction, the Japanese student is described as "now formulating a wireless method of transmission by which he hopes to electrocute the entire Russian forces. He is at present experimenting on Karchoff [the Bulgarian study-abroad senior] as the nearest substitute for a Russian."[9] Although the statement is obviously meant in jest, this description was written around the same time that the Russo-Japanese War was taking place, suggesting that either there is some truth to the statement and Sukichi may have actually disliked Russians, or that the writers of the *Debris* were drawing upon the world events of their time to form parallels with their own fellow students and make a generalized and stereotypical statement for the sole purpose of humor.[10]

Although the *Debris* categorizes him as "foreign," it would seem that Sukichi, as a student and member of the college community, was at least moderately active on campus and was well known by his peers. For example, he took a role in the Mechanics Burning, a traditional ceremony amongst Purdue students at the time.[11] Sukichi gave a reading at the ceremony, and the fact that he participated in an event in which there were few major presentations shows that he was accepted as a socially involved student. However, on the page in the 1904 *Debris* describing the Mechanics Burning, it was remarked that "Yoshisaka read a mixture of Japanese and pidgin English which no one understood," showing that the student body had no qualms about misrepresenting and insulting cultural differences that they viewed as oddities.[12]

Another example of how Sukichi was perceived by his peers occurs, again, in the 1904 *Debris*, in a poem titled "What Would You Think." The work consists of naming various students at Purdue and reciting for each person an activity that presumably would be considered by their peers to be absurdly incompatible with their own personalities and characters if they were to perform such actions. Sukichi is mentioned in this poem with the line "[What would you think if you should see] Sukichi called Smith."[13] The mere fact that he is mentioned in this poem suggests that Sukichi had enough of a noticeable presence on campus and among his fellow seniors to be given recognition as someone who was at least slightly popular, influential, or if nothing else, interesting. However, one also could claim that there is an underlying sense of mocking and even possibly racist sentiment toward Sukichi due to his heritage, as the poem seems to imply that a Japanese student possessing a common, predominantly Caucasian surname would be absurd and ridiculous. Such instances in which Sukichi's peers mocked his culture can be seen as further evidence that perhaps Sukichi, no matter how well liked he may have been by his peers, was never fully accepted by the other students.

Overall, for Sukichi in particular, it seems that his status as a Japanese student studying abroad made him the subject of some jokes and taunting. In comparison to the jabs faced by other students, it is not obvious whether or not Sukichi was teased or bullied in significantly harsher ways or more frequently than his peers, and in fact, such jabs at him may have been a sign that his peers were comfortable enough with him to feel a sense of camaraderie. However, it should be noted that Sukichi was primarily picked on simply because of his "foreign" status, unlike his peers, who got picked on for their habits or quirks. The fact that he was from Japan, that he was not quite like the rest of them, was seen by the other students as Sukichi's most noticeable feature, and whether or not their opinion of it was favorable or unsavory, it was the one aspect of Sukichi on which they primarily focused.

Even in 1904, the idea of studying abroad was established, having been popularized sometime around the late nineteenth century. For example, Walton remarks in her book that there were about 8,375 students from foreign nations who were studying abroad in American colleges in 1922.[14] Furthermore, in "Pilgrims to Western Seats of Learning—China's First Educational Mission to the United States," Arthur G. Robinson states that in 1872, just a few decades before

Sukichi came to Purdue, a group of Chinese students was sent to study abroad in Hartford, Massachusetts. The group consisted of 120 boys who were between the ages of nine to thirteen, and they were the participants of history's first organized educational exchange of Chinese students to America.[15] While the situation of these boys is in a lot of ways different to Sukichi's, due to differences in their respective time periods, ages, levels of education, countries of origin, and locations of the institutions attended, I believe some parallels can be drawn between the two scenarios due to the fact that both subjects were Asians who were studying in America at a time when racism and anti-Asian sentiment were significantly more widely and freely expressed than in the present day.

In the case of the boys from the 1872 project, Robinson mentions that the Chinese students were allowed some freedom by their foster families to maintain their Asian lifestyles. The study claims that the boys were not forced to go to church or change their style of dress, and while some did do so, it was of their own volition.[16] In addition, a group of educators, of which President Noah Porter of Yale University and author Mark Twain were members, praised the project for allowing the foreign students to stay true to their cultural heritage while also exploring new horizons, showing that there was a favorable and optimistic opinion about the future of the boys and the program amongst some intellectuals.[17] However, American society overall, and many academic institutions in particular, were not as easily accepting of the Asian students, as there was a widely spread attitude of racial stigma, especially on the Pacific Coast. When some of the Chinese boys attempted to apply for admittance to universities in Washington, they were soundly refused, with the reason for the rejection being "There is no room provided for Chinese students." This instance of rejection by the American universities was one of the biggest blows to the Chinese government's perception of the credibility and usefulness of the project, and in 1881, the students were recalled to China.[18] Once they returned, they faced disrespect from the Chinese populace and government simply because they had taken part in the project. Yet despite the circumstances, many of the boys grew to claim influential and well-respected positions in society as a result of their education abroad. These occupations included those of doctors, translators, government officials, and engineers.[19]

While Sukichi was from Japan rather than China and did not face the same sort of political backlash from his own home country, perhaps his situation did parallel that of the Chinese boys; perhaps he was given some grief by both American and Japanese society. As previously evidenced, there is reason to believe that Sukichi, while not necessarily bullied or greatly disrespected, was likely treated differently than his white American peers and stereotyped to a degree. Due to his Asian heritage, his fellow students were likely unable to fully accept him as being just like the rest of them, and similarly, his peers in Japan might not have been fully able to accept Sukichi due to his global experiences. His archival trail runs cold from this point forward, as I have not been able to locate American records of him beyond 1904. It is possible that Sukichi moved back to his hometown of Kobe, Japan, soon after graduating, and we may ponder whether, once back in his home country, he was yet again seen as somehow being different from the people around him, simply because he had studied in America. Studying abroad remained a controversial topic throughout Sukichi's time at Purdue and beyond. According to Chiang Yung-Chen in her article "Chinese Students in America in the Early Twentieth Century," Chinese dissenters of study-abroad programs in 1920 often stated that Western education and customs had no place in Eastern society and used such an argument to support their position.[20] Similarly, perhaps Sukichi was, in Japan, seen as somehow "foreign" for having learned English and possibly picked up American habits. Perhaps his newly acquired skills from college were dismissed on the basis that they had no place in Japanese society. Or perhaps, on the other hand, similar to the Chinese boys from 1872, his experience studying overseas actually made him a more ideal candidate for high-paying and well-respected jobs, and a degree in engineering from an American institution like Purdue might have made Sukichi seem like a more favorable candidate in the eyes of a Japanese employer.

Nowadays, Purdue sports a large population of international students on campus, and as of the fall 2013 semester, it ranks second amongst all public universities in terms of the number of international students enrolled.[21] Yet in 1904, Sukichi Yoshisaka was one of the very few on campus. In a time when international student programs were still coming into their own and racist attitudes ran more rampant, Sukichi can serve as an example of how study-abroad students lived in America at the turn of the twentieth century. Perhaps, by studying similar cases of international students throughout American history, we can even offer insight as to how views on international students have changed and evolved up until today.

Bibliography

"A Letter from Professor Robertson," *Exponent* (West Lafayette, IN), Sept. 23, 1903.

Chiang, Yung-Chen. "Chinese Students in America in the Early Twentieth Century." *Chinese Studies in History* 36, no. 3 (Spring 2003): 38.

"The Egyptian Vases." *Exponent* (West Lafayette, IN), Sept. 16, 1903.

"International Students and Scholars—Purdue University." Purdue University. Accessed November 12, 2013. http://www.iss.purdue.edu.

"Mister Kinnigan Tells of His 'Soonday Axkurshun'." *Exponent* (West Lafayette, IN), Sept. 23, 1903.

Purdue *Debris*. 1904. The Virginia Kelly Karnes Archives and Special Collections Research Center, Purdue University Libraries.

Robinson, Arthur G. "Pilgrims to Western Seats of Learning—China's First Educational Mission to the United States." *Chinese Studies in History* 36, no. 4 (Summer 2003): 65.

Walton, Whitney. *Internationalism, National Identities, and Study Abroad: France and the United States, 1890–1970*. Palo Alto, CA: Stanford University Press, 2010.

Notes

1. *Debris*, 1904, the Virginia Kelly Karnes Archives and Special Collections Research Center, Purdue University Libraries, 119.

2. "The Egyptian Vases," *Exponent* (West Lafayette, IN), Sept. 16, 1903, 3–4.

3. "Mister Kinnigan Tells of His 'Soonday Axkurshun'," *Exponent* (West Lafayette, IN), Sept. 23, 1903, 3–4.

4. "A Letter from Professor Robertson," *Exponent* (West Lafayette, IN), Sept. 23, 1903, 6.

5. *Debris*, 1904, 89.

6. Ibid., 93.

7. Ibid.

8. Whitney Walton, *Internationalism, National Identities, and Study Abroad: France and the United States, 1890–1970* (Palo Alto, CA: Stanford University Press, 2010), 2.

9. *Debris*, 1904, 119.

10. The Russo-Japanese War took place from February 1904 to September 1905. The cause was that both the Japanese and Russian empires wanted control of Manchuria.

11. The Mechanics Burning was an end-of-year ceremony at Purdue in which students burned their mechanics textbooks in a mock funeral.

12. *Debris*, 1904, 276.

13. Ibid., 300.

14. Walton, 1.

15. Arthur G. Robinson, "Pilgrims to Western Seats of Learning—China's First Educational Mission to the United States," *Chinese Studies in History* 36, no. 4 (Summer 2003): 63.

16. Ibid., 79.

17. Ibid., 83.

18. Ibid., 82.

19. Ibid., 86.

20. Yung-Chen Chiang, "Chinese Students in America in the Early Twentieth Century," *Chinese Studies in History* 36, no. 3 (Spring 2003): 40.

21. "International Students and Scholars—Purdue University," *Purdue University,* accessed November 12, 2013, http://www.iss.purdue.edu.

Lyla Vivian Marshall Harcoff: The Pursuits of a Small-Town Dreamer

 *Carolyn Griffith*

THE NAME Lyla Vivian Marshall is one to associate with passion, and on first read, her life is simply fantastic, full of excitement, and enviable. However, the story of Lyla is not just a shadow to be illuminated, but an example of hope. Exploring a Native American Mesa, moving to Chicago to pursue art full-time, studying abroad in Paris, and opening her own gallery in California all demonstrate Lyla's intentional attitude toward life. Lyla was one of the most interesting and successful members of the class of 1904, yet information about her life is hard to find—her fullest biography comes not from art historians or other scholars, but is published on the website of a gallery that carries her work.[1] She exemplified the life of a beautiful exception because she lived beyond fear to pursue her dreams, disregarding pessimism, pursuing hope, and making her small-town dreams a reality.

At first glance, the memories of Oak Lawn in Lafayette, Indiana, the childhood farm of Lyla, epitomize classic rural agrarian society in the late nineteenth and early twentieth centuries. A closer look, however, reveals inklings toward a slightly unconventional atmosphere. Gravel roads at Oak Lawn are the first indication that the farm was out of the ordinary. During major storms only those fortunate enough to have added gravel to their driveways were able to leave their homes, as opposed to those with dirt driveways who were forced to wait out the drying process. Furthermore, according to an early family historian, the Marshalls stocked a library "far more excellent than the library" of even a city home.[2] The man of the house, George Linley, thought beyond his life as a farmer and tinkered with the more scientific approaches to agrarian life. Consequently, he became involved in the experimental matters at Purdue University and became increasingly knowledgeable about the agricultural sciences of the time.[3] Could the irregular emphasis on formal education in the Marshall household have prompted Lyla to think beyond cultural expectations? George had a fairly simple education until he took matters into his own hands, acted on his ambition, and partnered with Purdue to gain beneficial knowledge to aid the community. Perhaps the expansive Marshall library led Lyla toward the life of the "New Woman" and the search for a home beyond her childhood farm's pastures.[4] Her father's experimental quest for knowledge seemed to have fostered a deep appreciation for intellect in this young farm girl and pushed Lyla toward independence.

Lyla made her first documented step toward personal independence with the pursuit of higher education by enrolling at Purdue University and joining the class of 1904.[5] Though she was initially from Oak Lawn in the Lafayette area, the move to West Lafayette and life on campus opened up a new world for young Lyla.[6] This uncommon choice of pursuing higher education at a time when it was not an expectation for women is even more noteworthy when considering that Lyla had an older brother, Linley Marshall.[7] Linley, though two years older, did not move to Purdue University until he followed Lyla's footsteps and joined the graduating class of 1905.[8]

At the start of her college career, Lyla dabbled, as current college students do. She tinkered with her interests until she solidified her true passion of art. The 1904 *Debris* lists her as a member of the Philalethean Literary Society her freshman through junior years. As a freshman, she served as a literary society critic and secretary. Not until her senior year did Lyla find her calling as an artist on the *Debris* staff. Though Lyla's family described her as having artistic interests from early childhood, inspired by the beautiful surroundings of Oak Lawn, Lyla truly seems to have discovered and honed her interests while in college. Her time at Purdue University was a time of friendship and self-discovery, similar to the experience of current college students. Lyla graduated with a bachelor's in science and a focus in art, a surprising achievement considering art was not offered at Purdue University as a formal course of study in 1904.[9] Lyla entered the University as a student and emerged as an artist, with her senior thesis on the topic of French Impressionism.[10]

Many themes of college life remain consistent, and Lyla faced the same kind of discrimination in the 1900s as anyone exceptional or different might still experience in the twenty-first century. Lyla was one of eight women in the class of 1904, a class of around 230 students. The men of the class were not overly hospitable to the entrance of women to the University, and this coed tension may have been a major force encouraging Lyla to join the Philalethean Society. The Philalethean Society was the premier women's debating society at Purdue University and a social safe haven for women at the predominantly male university. Weekly meetings afforded the female members a place of mental exercise and community.[11] Not only was the club beneficial for forming friendships, but it also aided in helping to form well-rounded women at a technical institute like Purdue. The Philalethean Society undoubtedly aided Lyla by creating an atmosphere of inclusion at the University, not only for her character, but also for her slightly off-kilter interests as compared to the athletic and mechanical or agricultural focus of the male-dominated student body.

Upon graduation in 1904, Lyla listed in the *Debris* her intention of furthering her art education at the Art Institute of Chicago, and true to her word, Lyla followed through on her plans. She enrolled in the Art Institute for two years and, as she grew more active in the art scene, journeyed to the Académie de Paris to continue her education.[12] She took three separate stints abroad in 1905, 1907, and 1912—another unusual choice for a time period when many of her friends were settling down and starting families.[13] She did not allow the fear of danger or traveling alone hinder the pursuit of her true passion—art. Lyla exemplified independence, and undoubtedly gained incomparable insight into the art world through her journeys.

A whirlwind of a woman, the young Lyla found herself in Chicago with years of artistic experience and no opportunity to practice her passion. According to an interview with her daughter, Jane Martindale, Lyla painted ceramics at Marshall Fields and Company in Chicago as a fine arts designer. Lyla desired to practice her honed artistic talent but was unable to find work teaching, so she intentionally pursued art with the only job available to her in the Marshall Fields fine arts department.[14] Once more Lyla centered herself in a new, major artistic trend. Large department stores had begun to install fine arts departments to offer handcrafted merchandise and, in the Chicago area especially, many fledgling artists from the Art Institute were hired for work.[15]

Lyla worked at Marshall Fields for close to a year to accrue two weeks of vacation time.[16] With the time, she fancied a trip out West and bought a train ticket. Her two-week trip grew into over two months away from home, as Lyla on a whim stepped off the train at a station in Winslow, Arizona, and took a pack train out to the Second Mesa, one of three mesas upon which the Hopi Indians centered their civilizations.[17] Pack trains, or lines of animals, were used on especially difficult terrain. The 1914 Purdue *Alumnus* reports that Lyla "mounted to the Second Mesa of Hopiland" where she summered, sketching and painting the native culture until the change of seasons.[18] Her trip culminated in the creation of six finalized, beautiful canvases.[19] Lyla's summer with the tribe allotted her a deeper connection with the native lifestyles, reflected in many of her later works.

According to Jane, the story neared the more fantastic realm as Lyla packed up her belongings toward the end of the summer, intending to take the train. Her return stub only allowed her one seat, and a nameless conductor informed Lyla that she would need to buy a second ticket for her paintings. Unable to afford a ticket, Lyla remained undaunted and slept through the night in a shelter of her own paintings, weathering a rather untimely storm in a shield of canvas. Upon the train's return the next day, the conductor was shocked to see the woman had survived the night alone. The powerful symbol of womanhood impressed even Mr. Ripley, the CEO of the Atchison, Topeka, and Santa Fe Railroad line, who coincidentally seemed to be riding the train that very day.[20] Ripley purchased two of her paintings on the spot, perhaps as impressed with her spunk and tenacity as he was with her artistic ability, and allowed Lyla to continue her journey in spite of the miserly conductor.[21]

In this way, Lyla was once more flung into the beginning of an art movement. Just a few years earlier the Atchison, Topeka, and Santa Fe Railroad line had developed an interest in art acquisition. Encouraging eastern artists to paint native western tribes, the company began commissioning artwork in 1892 and then used the paintings on calendars or advertisements for westward movement in the early 1900s.[22] The calendars truly began to gain popularity about the time of Lyla's stint in Arizona, and they remained desirable through the middle of the century.[23]

Proving facts of the beautiful tale is a difficult task; however, several clues allow a layer of doubt to be whittled away. According to the Sullivan Goss Gallery, which carries Lyla's paintings today, the remaining paintings from that summer have tide marks marring the back of the canvas. The gallery explains the origin of these marks as due to a severe soaking of the canvas.[24] Not only do the tide marks point to the truth of the tale, but an old Purdue *Alumnus* clipping also mentions Lyla's work, "Moonlight in Mishongnovi," as purchased by the Santa Fe Railroad.[25] Additionally, *Artists in California, 1786-1940* lists Lyla's work as displayed in a Santa Fe Railroad art exhibit.[26] The story of her overnight stay on the railroad platform seems plausible, given Lyla's determined character.

Though her next trip is only briefly mentioned in the Purdue alumni magazine, Lyla received the honor in 1914 to join "a small party of artists to take a six weeks' sketching trip through Estes Park, Colo., the Yellowstone Park, and Shoshone Canyon as a guest of the Burlington railroad."[27] Perhaps her trip served as an advertising technique for the newly expanding railroad line to stay competitive.[28]

She lived a busy lifestyle, refraining from settling but remaining attached to the University after her graduation in 1904. Lyla proved her dedication to Purdue by subscribing to the Purdue *Alumnus* upon the magazine's initial publication. She even carved the time out of her busy schedule in 1914 to return for the Purdue Alumni Day and visit her colleagues once more.[29] Purdue University was evidently very dear to Lyla, and as she grew more practiced in her art, she even donated several paintings to the University. Two paintings were donated specifically for Fowler Hall: one of Rural Route 1, and a second of Rip Van Winkle, which was placed in the College Inn in 1914.[30]

Though Lyla's choice of Purdue may have been initially tied to her father's experimental interests at the University, the decision to pursue higher education should earn Lyla a good deal of respect. Higher education was not a practical necessity for women in the early 1900s—especially for Lyla, who no doubt was busy enough on the family farm. Lyla's step of attending Purdue University set her apart from just a small-town dreamer and pushed Lyla to reach her childhood aspirations.

In 1916, Lyla married Constantine Harcoff, a Russian engineer.[31] Lyla made the choice to take on her husband's name in spite of all the work she had done building up the name of "Lyla Marshall" in the art community. Though Lyla was a self-made woman, cultural patterns still swayed her lifestyle, and to maintain a maiden name or hyphenate both names as is currently common was nearly unheard of at the time.[32] The couple lived together in Chicago for several years, but it was still too early for Lyla to fathom settling down, even after Jane arrived. The small family moved to Santa Barbara in 1927, and Lyla served as the artist managing director of the Balcony Gallery at 29 East de la Guerra Street.[33] *The Argus,* a critical art magazine, mentions Lyla as having the most "striking" painting at an exhibit, proving Lyla had the artistic skill to be competitive in the industry.[34] Lyla was actively involved in the Santa Barbara art scene upon the family's move and joined the Art League of Santa Barbara.[35]

The mid-1930s once more catapulted Lyla into the hub of art and culture, working through the Great Depression with many famous counterparts for the Federal Art Project (FAP), a branch of the Second Deal Works Progress Administration. The program encouraged art appreciation and supported many young artists before they later reached fame. Since Lyla worked in the Mural Division, she may have had the opportunity to work alongside a young Jackson Pollock or Arshile Gorky.[36] Lyla is credited as the author of three murals for the Santa Ynez High School.[37] One of the murals is of Native American influence, possibly a reflection of her time spent with the Hopi tribe in her younger years.

By 1941, the FAP was winding down and facing budget cuts in the face of World War II, but Lyla had already sensed the changing tides and moved on to build her own studio.[38] She asked a strong, independent contemporary of the time, Lutah Mariah Riggs, to rework an old carriage house into a studio and living quarters. Lutah was one of the nation's first female architects and more specifically the very first woman with an architect's license in Santa Barbara. She lived the lifestyle of a woman of independence, even compared to today's standards. She never married, preferring to balance several part-time jobs and pursue her passions. Though scorned as a woman in her field, even by a partner at her firm, Lutah proved herself and her skill and established quite a following, designing unique styles inspired by exotic foreign cultures.[39] Her patrons ranged from locals to Hollywood movie stars.[40]

It is possible to imagine the kindred relationship that may have formed between these two women who did not fit the mold of their era. Each pushed boundaries and practiced her art form with skill and irrepressible vitality. Lutah helped Lyla design the studio of her dreams, with a bit of humor. Retrofitting an old carriage house, the phrase "Adios Caballos," or "Goodbye Horses," danced in the doorway.[41]

In 1956, after years of travel and excitement, Lyla said good-bye to her family and passed away. A woman of determination, she instilled that quality in Jane, who petitioned for their home in Santa Barbara to become a historical monument.[42]

Starting her young life with the choice of Purdue University and higher education, Lyla swam against the cultural current and societal dictates to passionately pursue her goals. She acted intentionally, demonstrating strength of character and a nearly infectious vitality for life that seemed to parallel passion. Lyla metamorphosed from a small-town farm girl into a high-fashion Californian gallery director. To learn from the life of such an irrepressible woman is a beautiful opportunity afforded to those who follow. However, she lived more than an interesting life. Lyla Vivian

Marshall Harcoff may have been a cultural anomaly, but she demonstrated the power of determination and hope by achieving so much beyond the usual realm of possibility.

Bibliography

Art Institute of Chicago. *Catalogue of the First Exhibition of Works by the Alumni of the Art Institute of Chicago*. Chicago: Art Institute of Chicago, 1918. http://www.artic.edu/sites/default/files/libraries/pubs/1918/AIC1918SAICAlumni_comb.pdf.

Bardach, Ann Louise. "Shangra-La." *LA Yoga Magazine* 9, no. 3 (2010). http://layogamagazine.com/content/index.php?option=com_content&view=article&id=566%3Ashangri-la&catid=160%3Aapril-2010-issue&Itemid=55.

California State Library (1906). *News Notes of California Libraries*. Sacramento, CA: California State Library.

Cowell, Pattie. "'Strong, and Wild, and Green': Ethel Augur's Western Adventure, 1911-1914." *Legacy: A Journal of American Women Writers* 24, no. 1 (2007): 93.

Dye, Victoria E. *All Aboard for Santa Fe: Railway Promotion of the Southwest, 1890s to 1930s*. Albuquerque: University of New Mexico Press, 2005.

"Early College Women: Determined to be Educated." Accessed November 12, 2013. http://www.northnet.org/stlawrenceaauw/profiles.htm.

"Federal Art Project in Northern Southern California, Mural Decorations—Completed and in Progress." http://www.wpamurals.com.

Fried, Stephen. *Appetite for America: How Visionary Businessman Fred Harvey Built a Railroad Hospitality Empire that Civilized the Wild West*. New York: Bantam Books, 2010.

Goldin, C., and M. Shim. "Making a Name: Women's Surnames at Marriage and Beyond." *Journal of Economic Perspectives* 18, no. 2 (2004): 143–160.

Goss, Frank. "Lyla Vivian Marshall Harcoff: The Sale of Her First Paintings as a Professional Artist." December 22, 2008. http://sullivangossblog.site.aplus.net/blog/?p=56.

"Hopi Tribe." *Inter Tribal Council of Arizona, Inc.* 2011. http://itcaonline.com/?page_id=1162.

Hughes, E. M. *Artists in California, 1786-1940*. Sacramento, CA: Crocker Art Museum, 2002.

Lapin, Claudia. "Lutah Mariah Riggs: Local Legend of Architecture." *Santa Barbara Seasons* (blog), August 29, 2013. http://sbseasons.com/blog/lutah-maria-riggs-local-legend-of-architecture/.

"Lyla Marshall Harcoff." *Sullivan Goss*. 2010. http://www.sullivangoss.com/lyla_harcoff/.

"Lyla Vivian Marshall." Purdue *Debris*. 1904. The Virginia Kelly Karnes Archives and Special

Collections Research Center, Purdue University Libraries.

Marshall, Wallace. *A History of the Marshall and Related Families*. Edited by Frances Maude Spaits. Lafayette, IN: Haywood Publishing, 1922.

Mavigliano, George. "The Federal Art Project: Holger Cahill's Program of Action." *Art Education* 37, no. 3 (1984): 26–30.

"The Philalethean Society." Purdue *Debris*. 1901. The Virginia Kelly Karnes Archives and Special Collections Research Center, Purdue University Libraries.

Rodenberger, Joan. "Lafayette *Journal and Courier* Newspaper Index, 1902-1952." 2003. http://www.ingenweb.org/intippecanoe/JC_mam.html.

Salinger, Jehane B. "Women Artists Exhibit at Santa Barbara Art League." *The Argus* III, 3 (1928). San Francisco Public Library Digitization. https://archive.org/details/argus1192751929sali.

"Santa Fe Calendar History." Accessed November 11, 2013. http://dlbriscoe.com/santa-fe-railway-calendars.html.

Warren, Lynne. *Art*. Accessed November 9, 2013. http://www.encyclopedia.chicagohistory.org/pages/72.html.

Weigle, Frederic H. 1934. Purdue *Alumni Directory* (1875-1934). The Virginia Kelly Karnes Archives and Special Collections Research Center, Purdue University Libraries.

Wolf, Justin. *The Federal Art Project of the Works Progress Administration WPA*. Accessed November 11, 2013. http://www.theartstory.org/org-wpa.htm.

Notes

1. "Lyla Marshall Harcoff," *Sullivan Goss,* 2010, http://www.sullivangoss.com/lyla_harcoff/.

2. Wallace Marshall, *A History of the Marshall and Related Families*, ed. Frances Maude Spaits (Lafayette, IN: Haywood Publishing, 1922).

3. Ibid.

4. Ibid.

5. "Lyla Vivian Marshall," Purdue *Debris*, 1904, the Virginia Kelly Karnes Archives and Special Collections Research Center, Purdue University Libraries.

6. Marshall, *History of the Marshall and Related Families*.

7. In 1900, only 2.8 percent of the female population went to college. "Early College Women: Determined to be Educated," accessed November 12, 2013, http://www.northnet.org/stlawrenceaauw/profiles.htm.

8. Linley died in 1907 from typhoid fever after studying engineering at Purdue University. Wallace Marshall, *A History of the Marshall and Related Families*.

9. Frank Goss, "Lyla Vivian Marshall Harcoff: The Sale of Her First Paintings as a Professional Artist," December 22, 2008, http://sullivangossblog.site.aplus.net/blog/?p=56.

10. *Debris*, 1904.

11. "The Philalethean Society," Purdue *Debris,* 1901, the Virginia Kelly Karnes Archives and Special Collections Research Center, Purdue University Libraries.

12. E. M. Hughes, *Artists in California, 1786-1940* (Ann Arbor: Sheridan Books, 2002).

13. "Lyla Marshall Harcoff," *Sullivan Goss*.

14. Goss, "Lyla Vivian Marshall Harcoff."

15. Lynne Warren, *Art,* http://www.encyclopedia.chicagohistory.org/pages/72.html.

16. Goss, "Lyla Vivian Marshall Harcoff."

17. "Hopi Tribe: Introductory Information," *Inter Tribal Council of Arizona*, 2011, http://itcaonline.com/?page_id=1162.

18. For future study on the experience of a lone woman traveler to the West in the 1910s, Ethel Augur's experience complements Lyla's journey well. Ethel Augur narrated her journey through a series of letters to her family. Pattie Cowell, "'Strong, and Wild, and Green': Ethel Augur's Western Adventure, 1911-1914." *Legacy: A Journal of American Women Writers* 24, no. 1 (2007): 93.

19. Purdue *Alumnus* II (1914), the Virginia Kelly Karnes Archives and Special Collections Research Center, Purdue University Libraries.

20. Goss, "Lyla Vivian Marshall Harcoff."

21. Ibid.

22. Victoria E. Dye, *All Aboard for Santa Fe: Railway Promotion of the Southwest, 1890s to 1930s* (Albuquerque: University of New Mexico Press, 2005).

23. "Santa Fe Calendar History," http://dlbriscoe.com/santa-fe-railway-calendars.html.

24. Goss, "Lyla Vivian Marshall Harcoff."

25. Purdue *Alumnus* VI (1919), the Virginia Kelly Karnes Archives and Special Collections Research Center, Purdue University Libraries.

26. Hughes, "Artists in California," 2002.

27. Purdue *Alumnus* VI (1919).

28. For more information on the highly competitive nature of the railroad lines in the early 1900s, see the life of Fred Harvey, an entrepreneur managing the food services and eventual resorts in the growing West. Stephen Fried, *Appetite for America: How*

Visionary Businessman Fred Harvey Built a Railroad Hospitality Empire that Civilized the Wild West (New York: Bantam Books, 2010).

29. Purdue *Alumnus* II (1914).

30. Purdue *Alumnus* VI (1919).

31. Joan Rodenberger, "Lafayette *Journal and Courier* Newspaper Index, 1902-1952," 2003, http://www.ingenweb.org/intippecanoe/JC_mam.html.

32. Lucy Stone, married in 1855, is the earliest recorded example of a woman keeping her maiden name. The Lucy Stone League, in honor of Lucy Stone, devoted efforts to help women retain personal identities in the late nineteenth and early twentieth centuries. A study by Harvard focusing on Harvard alumni listed 4 percent of women as keeping their names after being married in 1975. C. Goldin and M. Shim, "Making a Name: Women's Surnames at Marriage and Beyond," *Journal of Economic Perspectives* 18, no. 2 (2004): 143-60.

33. Frederic H. Weigle, Purdue *Alumni Directory* (1875-1934). The Virginia Kelly Karnes Archives and Special Collections Research Center, Purdue University Libraries.

34. Jehane B. Salinger, "Women Artists Exhibit at Santa Barbara Art League," *The Argus* III, 3 (1928). San Francisco Public Library Digitization, https://archive.org/details/argus1192751929sali.

35. Hughes, "Artists in California," 2002.

36. Justin Wolf, *The Federal Art Project of the Works Progress Administration WPA*, http://www.theartstory.org/org-wpa.htm.

37. Federal Art Project in Northern Southern California, Mural Decorations—Completed and in Progress, http://www.wpamurals.com.

38. George Mavigliano, "The Federal Art Project: Holger Cahill's Program of Action," *Art Education* 37, no. 3 (1984): 26–30.

39. One remarkable design by Riggs was a temple and yoga studio inspired by ancient South Indian temples. She designed the temple and conferred with Frank Lloyd Wright for the landscaping design. Ann Louise Bardach, Shangra-La," *LA Yoga Magazine* 9, no. 3 (2010), http://layogamagazine.com/content/index.php?option=com_content&view=article&id=566%3Ashangri-la&catid=160%3Aapril-2010-issue&Itemid=55.

40. Claudia Lapin, "Lutah Mariah Riggs: Local Legend of Architecture," *Santa Barbara Seasons* (blog), August 29, 2013, http://sbseasons.com/blog/lutah-maria-riggs-local-legend-of-architecture/.

41. City of Santa Barbara. Martindale Residence, 220 East Pueblo Street, September 11, 2013.

42. Ibid.

"The Eternal Feminine": An Examination of the Life and Times of the Twentieth-Century New University Woman through Cecil Clare Crane

Cedar Marie Woodworth

ON A TWENTIETH century, midwestern land-grant college campus where physical vigor, scientific investigation, upstanding moral conduct, and athletic prowess were chief concerns of the culture and measures of success, where does a literary mind, more importantly, that of a woman, find her place? Who was Cecil Clare Crane of Bryan, Ohio? Posing this question is akin to asking a much larger one: Who was the "new university woman" at the turn of the twentieth century and what traditional roles or alternative subcultures may she have embraced? In what ways did she work to subvert or perpetuate gender norms? Who were her friends, companions, and lovers during this period of great change in our nation's history? Using Cecil as a lens and representation of the new university woman, I am looking specifically to describe and speculate about aspects of her personal life and the experiences she and her fellow female classmates, or "coeds," had at Purdue University. Through representations of close readings of primary archival materials, I will detail several snapshots of Cecil's life. These sections will include an introduction of Cecil, portraits of life in the women's residence hall and literary societies at Purdue, and the relevance of Cecil's senior thesis on the illustrious French woman, George Sand. Finally, coming full circle, I will describe the implications of post-university life, explaining Cecil's existence as a seeming "every woman." Cecil Clare Crane was a student, a woman, a literary scholar, a mother, and a wife. She embodies an entire stratum of her generation. She is a thousand women; she is me, and she may very well be you.

Who Was the New Woman?

At the turn of the century, a "new" type of woman was emerging. New women "conducted themselves with a new independence and assertiveness . . . by shopping in department stores, smoking in public, playing tennis, expressing interest in sexuality, earning advanced degrees, entering traditionally male professions, calling for social and political reforms, or agitating for the ballot. Self-development, not self-sacrifice, was the New Woman's watchword."[1] Cecil and other coeds at Purdue University and across the country helped usher in this new generation of women who held themselves to higher standards of education, awareness, and opportunity. Seen as revolutionaries by some and headaches by others, these women were both celebrated and harshly denounced. In a satirical take on those who feared the New Woman, Purdue's student newspaper, the *Exponent*, reflects several criticisms in a story in which the "horrors" of those who "turn out to be coeds" are described. Such women "lose their dignity and womanliness, they take up the coarse ways of the boys, they use slang and chew gum and wear box-calf shoes and short skirts and rain-coats and toboggan caps and—and they sit on the bleachers at the games and jump up and yell—think of it! . . . they study Physics and Mathematics and Chemistry and work in laboratories."[2] Facing these judgments and perceptions, new women strove to gain independence and succeed academically and physically, while still remaining socially acceptable.

Cecil Clare Crane

Cecil Clare Crane, the daughter of Francis H. and Samuel Crane, a bookkeeper, was born in Bryan, Ohio, on October 20, 1883. Around 1891, Cecil and her family relocated to Lafayette, Indiana, where she attended the city high school, eventually entering Purdue University in the fall of 1900 as a freshman member of the class of 1904. During her time at the University, Cecil was an integral part of literary Purdue, and as her *Debris* yearbook cameo states, she was "one of our esteemed." Cecil was also involved in the Philalethean Literary Society, Purdue's newspaper (the *Exponent*), and the production of the 1904 *Debris*. In the campus tradition of bestowing titles upon seniors, she was crowned winner of the "funny girl" contest and runner-up in the "laziest girl event."[3] Featured alongside many of her classmates in a piece of anecdotal verse crafted to incorporate their names, she was described as a "solitary CRANE."[4] Cecil is also noted in the *Debris* as having "a lively spirit of humor . . . [she liked] to take a shy at her classmates in the form of roast."[5]

"Art of Entertaining" by the Hall Girls

Ladies' Hall, constructed in 1872 as Boarding Hall, was the first building on campus erected north of State Street. It was originally home to the college dining room, faculty living quarters, and president's office when Purdue opened its doors in September 1874. The building was also known for a time as Art Hall when

FIGURE 1. LADIES' HALL ON A SUNNY DAY. COURTESY OF PURDUE LIBRARIES ARCHIVES AND SPECIAL COLLECTIONS.

various drawing and cooking classes were taught in some of the rooms on the first floor. However, for the majority of its existence, it was used as the women's residence hall. All of the coeds living on campus in 1904, including Cecil, resided here. Ladies' Hall was much more than a simple dormitory; it was the stoic witness of personal and intellectual growth and the lighthearted antics and adventures of the hall girls and their companions.

In capturing the spirit of the University, the 1904 *Debris* features a section that playfully attributes hypothetical book titles to "student authors" in the class of 1904; one such selection is entitled "Art of

Figure 2. Cooking class in Ladies' Hall. Courtesy of Purdue Libraries Archives and Special Collections.

Figure 3. A group of coeds crowd together for a photo (*Debris* 1904, 254).

Entertaining" by the Hall Girls, and another is entitled "Cupid's Garden, or, The Back Yard of Ladies' Hall" by a pair of male students.[8] Well known for their hospitality and parties, the ladies gave "chafing dish luncheons" for visitors[9] and farewell dinners for departing female faculty members.[10] A group referred to as the "Basement Sisters" even "gave a birthday spread for Miss Crane [one] Wednesday."[11] After a fair amount of research, I am still only able to speculate about who the Basement Sisters may have been—perhaps a subset of the literary society or an intimate group of cohorts who assembled in the nether regions of Ladies' Hall. Either way, the community of Ladies' Hall women developed ardent relationships. As expressively characterized in the *Exponent*, each woman looked to the others for a soul who "thinks the same of you in sadness as in joy and one in whom your confidence is as firm as in your own self. One who laughs with you, and one who weeps with you. One who is as eager to sacrifice for you as you are for her and, finally, one who thinks with you and with whom you think."[12]

Out of these close bonds rose an affable culture, which included a few hall traditions. One of particular importance was the infamous "college girl's fudge." The crafting of college girl's fudge commenced with "a skirmish for alcohol"—as each suspiciously claimed that "mine has all evaporated"—followed by a "perfect serenity and rustle of skirts." The ever-popular chafing dish was then called to duty, "the scent of chocolate inspiring," as they gathered "all the sugar that could be gotten from boxes and sacks," and called for "butter, nuts, [and] dates, left from midnight feasts [to] come forth."[13] The fudge's elevated standing in women's college culture is depicted in the following 1904 *Debris* illustration entitled "An Engineer's Idea of a Girl's Head." The drawing features the typical thoughts of a coed. Fudge has a prominent place among her chief considerations, which also included theatre, traveling men, "clothes, lots of 'em," mathematics, polo, frat men, and "hair, more hair, preferably brunette."[14]

FIGURE 4. "AN ENGINEER'S IDEA OF A GIRL'S HEAD" (*DEBRIS* 1904, 301).

Aside from fulfilling traditionally feminine roles and stereotypes, the coeds also sought to establish a physical culture of their own in response to the increasing zeal for "real" masculinity and athleticism. Raising questions about the proposed construction of the new Memorial Gymnasium they asked, "will we find a place? . . . will there be no room that the Purdue girl can call her own, no room where we can meet for physical training and where we can have a basket ball team. . . . If Purdue is open to girls, should they not be offered inducements, outside of their studies, such as are given by other coeducational institutions?"[15] Their requests were apparently followed by action, as the following *Exponent* issue announced that, "The young women of the University have organized a physical culture class. . . . The 'coeds' are to be congratulated on their spirit of aggressiveness, as an effort last year to organize such a class was a total failure. The class enrolls almost every girl of the University. It is thought and hoped that a basket ball team will be started and a regular schedule will be made up with the different colleges over the state. Why shouldn't the girls, as well as the rest, hang athletic scalps in the library!"[16]

The spirit of the coeds and their escapades lived on right up until the demolition of Ladies' Hall in 1927. A couple of later highlights include an event in which some of the residents in the '20s dressed up as colonial

Figure 5. A group of coeds dressed in traditional colonial garb. Courtesy of Purdue Libraries Archives and Special Collections.

men and women, and another that led to a mysterious January 1913 *Exponent* article featuring the indelicate headline, "Coeds in Kimonos Clamber to Roofs and Put Out Fire."

Literary Life

Cecil, along with many of her fellow coeds, was very engaged with the literary culture at Purdue, and she worked as an editor for the *Exponent*, which began featuring a "Girls' Page" during her time on the staff. Cecil also worked with the Philalethean Literary Society, of which she was president, and as the literary editor in the 1904 production of the *Debris*.[17]

Commenting on Cecil's newspaper involvement, the *Debris* calls her "a wielder of the paste and shears," praising her for affording "entertainment for many by her apt selections for the exchange pages of the *Exponent*."[18] As the exchange editor, she was responsible for choosing small news clips from other college newspapers across the country to include in the *Exponent*. As a result, Cecil controlled some of the flow of information onto campus. We can get an impression of Cecil's voice from her various selections and commentary; through the pieces she found interesting enough to include, a sense of her humor and personality may be gleaned. One particular piece of humorous social commentary can be found in the December 3, 1903, exchange pages from an address about prominent Victorian art critic and theorist John Ruskin by Dr. Hillis in the *Ohio Wesleyan Transcript*: "The time is past when men can say that men alone work and think, and that 'man must work that women may spend.' Man is the most conceited form of biped that the world ever knew. He asks all the women in the universe to stand around and worship at his little shrine. There was a man in England by the name of Lord, who invented a tool. After inventing that tool, he signed himself Lord, Jr., to distinguish himself from the lord almighty –Ex."[19] This piece, signed "Ex"—presumably for "Exchange Editor"—amusingly jabs at antiquated gender roles while communicating a sense of change in attitudes toward women. On Purdue's campus, further development of the publication of women's voices can be seen in the advent of the "Girls' Page" in the *Exponent*, beginning in February 1904. Over many issues, the page covers a broad range of topics and seeks to recognize, distinguish, and strengthen the women's community on campus. One specific sentiment reflective of the slowly maturing recognition of feminine independence at Purdue states that, "Woman is, by nature, frail and timid and it is not her place to be out, unattended . . . " however, "Is this the state of affairs at Purdue? Most decidedly, it is not."[20]

Figure 6. The 1904 Philalethean Literary Society (*Debris* 1904, 196).

Many of the coeds were also involved in the Philalethean Literary Society, which was not only a lively source of literary discourse and expansion on campus, but also a key facet of social life at the University. Along with the Carlyle, Emersonian, and Irving male literary societies, the women held debates, balls, and joint meetings, which were sometimes opened up as spectacle to University students and faculty. During one such rendezvous between the Philalethean women and Irving men in mid-February 1904, the "conversationings" included poetry readings, piano duets, recitations, and a debate in which it was "Resolved: That Valentine Day should be perpetuated." Following the conclusion of the debate, refreshments were served, "consisting of ice cream, moulded in heart shaped form, with cake and candy."[22] The groups also hosted Literary Annuals each year during Gala Week, a time in which life was "supreme in every phase of interest" and about the college grounds was "the greatest spirit of good cheer and joyousness that may be imagined."[23]

George Sand in Indiana

In contrast to the seemingly lighthearted activities of the literary society, Cecil's senior thesis gives us a more earnest, personal sense of her through the close examination of its subject matter on the well-known French author, George Sand. Among other things, Sand's works challenge and explore the exclusion of women from the "masculinist discourse of politics," sexuality, principles of feminism, monogamy, class equality, and "the gendered conflict between idealism and realism."[24] Sand smoked cigarettes and had a long list of lovers; she was "reviled as a lesbian" and a "man-eater" and known for dressing in traditionally masculine clothing.[25]

FIGURE 7. AN 1864 PORTRAIT OF GEORGE SAND. COURTESY OF GEORGE EASTMAN HOUSE COLLECTION. AVAILABLE FROM GALLICA BIBLIOTHEQUE NUMÉRIQUE.

Literary subject matter was quite influential and, as reported in the *Exponent*, a lecture was given on campus stating that, "A book is valuable as a piece of literature just in proportion to its capability of entering into and becoming a part of one's life. Intelligence has, therefore, the same moment in choosing one's reading as in choosing one's friends."[26] With this notion in mind, Cecil may have found, in researching the author and characters featured in her senior thesis—*The Idealism of George Sand*—companions of sorts: like-minded women of extremely different circumstance with whom she shared the struggle of defining eternal femininity.

Cecil's forty-one-page thesis, handwritten in delicate script, begins with an introductory description of Sand. "She had a rare genius,"[27] Cecil wrote. "She had a receptive mind and infinitely good, she became the organ of all reforms, which seemed for the good of humanity . . . to see how great the influence of a woman can be . . . none can be more interesting than that of . . . George Sand."[28] After establishing this tone of praise, Cecil goes into much detail about Sand's life, casually describing several facets that would likely have been considered quite controversial. George Sand had a "dislike of conventional ideals"[29] and "she received no religious education whatever." Eventually, "she imagined a being who would represent all perfections, human and divine. To this being she gave the name 'Corambé,' and for several years she cherished this fantasy. She erected an alter in a thicket and there offered as sacrifice the release of birds and butterflies that had been taken as prisoners."[30] After mentioning Sand's period of self-conceived religiosity, Cecil describes Sand's early teenage years at the convent school she attended in Paris. Here Sand became "the leader of the gayety and of the set called the 'devils,' she herself earning the nickname of 'madcap.'"[31] Upon return to the French countryside, Sand broke up her daily responsibilities at home with "armless horseback rides" in which "she was fearless. [Sand] donned a boy's riding costume, which raised an outcry from the village folk . . . here it was [she] learned to look with contempt on the narrow restrictions laid down by the village social code."[32]

Such open challenges of standardized religion, modesty, and gender performance were also evident in Sand's writings. In particular, Cecil acclaims *Lélia*, a controversial work by Sand that follows a woman named Lélia who, as described by contemporary critics, "appears in some ways to be trapped in transition between the place of the traditional woman and that of the modern."[33] In this state of New Womanhood, Lélia is "trying to find a space in which she can exist as something other than the object of someone's desire, trying to find also her voice."[34] Cecil comments that, "*Lélia* is a strange, incoherent and magnificent poem, in which spirituality falls low and sensuality aspires high, where we pass from scenes of debauchery to lofty prayer and where inspiration rises high only to fall to the depths. Lélia is a mysterious heroine . . . into this book [Sand] claims she has put more of her own self than in any other work."[35] In these important analyses, Cecil finds commonality with her subjects. Arguably the most significant lines of the thesis are found when Cecil poignantly characterizes Sand's body of work as a whole, saying her pieces "show the fortune of the poor and great human heart, the conflict of the living soul with fate, the revolt of nature against the fatal errors of society; they protect against everything that shackles the free movement of true love. Each is a poem consecrated to divine love and human love and [Sand] says herself, 'they were written under a sway of emotion not of a system.'"[36]

Cecil's idealistic, methodical treatment of Sand's scandalous lifestyle, upbringing, and writings show that she herself may have been attracted to a subversive culture, or was at the very least comfortable with a woman's departure from traditional expectation. Discussing such unconventional topics in an idealistic manner reflects the changing interest of the New Woman and the progression of thought.

Graduation and Beyond

In the aforementioned section of the *Debris*, which attributes hypothetical book titles to students, Cecil also had work credited to her authorship—"Changed Heart"[37]—a title that perhaps comments on her appearance in the yearbook under the "Matrimonially Inclined" section in the "Lovelorn Damsels" category.[38] The object of her affection and cause for her change of heart was Walter H. Schulte, a dashing, athletic pharmacy student in the Purdue class of 1905. Schulte was "from the Evansville Dutch, and . . . [had] a liking for anything in petticoats, especially 'college widows.'" As defined by *Merriam-Webster Dictionary*, a college widow is "a young woman in a college town who dates students of successive college classes." Such may have been the case for Cecil, who was one year his senior. In addition, Schulte was also a member of the pharmacy football team (1904) and the pharmacy editor of the 1905 *Debris*.[39]

LOVELORN DAMSELS

"Man's best possession is a sympathetic wife."

Evelyn Allison	Lois Yager
Helen Darby	Ella Shearer
Cecil Crane	Lyla Marshall

FIGURE 8. THE "LOVELORN DAMSELS" AWARD (*DEBRIS* 1904, 298).

Cecil's *Debris* cameo ends with a brief statement saying, "When she finishes here she expects to indulge in school teaching for a time, unless—."[40] In this mysterious-sounding ending, I would like to think that Cecil was imagining herself in an expatriate literary group on the Left Bank in Paris, but undoubtedly, she means "unless—" she marries.

After graduation, Cecil did in fact "indulge" in teaching for a while in Lafayette, residing at 223 North Sixth Street from 1904 to mid-1912, presumably continuing her courtship with Walter, whose 1905 *Debris* cameo fittingly states, "his favorite resort is Sixth Street, and it is not difficult to tell which end of it."[41] Census data indicates that Walter returned to Evansville, Indiana, after graduating in 1905 and began work as a pharmacist, eventually opening his own pharmacy, called W. H. Schulte Drug Co., sometime between 1912 and 1916. Cecil appears to have continued teaching in Lafayette up until the end of the school year in 1912, presumably moving to Evansville over the summer. She and Walter were married on October 29, 1912. The review of periodic censuses and several Purdue *Register of Offices and Alumni* yield similar information for the coming decades: "Mr. W. H. Schulte, PhG, and Mrs. W. H. Schulte: Homemaker" lived at 1519 East Delaware Street in Evansville, just a few

Figure 9. Senior portrait of Walter Hugo Schulte (*Debris* 1904, 132).

residences down from the pharmacy, which was located at 1521 East Delaware Street. The Schultes had three children: Walter Crane (b. 1914), Frances Ann (b. 1918), and Betty Clare (b. 1921).

When I eventually reached the *Register* entry that listed Cecil as "deceased," I felt a surprising amount of sadness. I came to the sharp realization that in a matter of hours, I had covered the statistical entirety of a woman's life. Despite the bare sketch of her life that we can construct from archival records, through her contributions to the *Exponent*, and her extensive senior thesis, I felt that I had also gained an impression of who she was, or at least, a sense of her humor, interests, and some values of personal importance. While trying to understand the connection I felt, I was attempting to explain the positions of archival obscurity in which Cecil and many other university women eventually found themselves when I suddenly understood: these women did not simply "find" themselves in some condition; they embodied, to the best of their abilities and talents, the circumstances that they were allowed. As the women themselves reflect in the *Exponent*, "Woman's influence over man is supreme. She made Ceasar [*sic*] fall at her feet while the armies of the world trembled before him," and her "greatest influence is exerted in the home. It is there she wields such a mighty influence in shaping the destiny of the world. It is there that the individuals who compose the nation are nurtured and when they gain in power and influence, the nation must likewise be strong and prosperous."[42] This notion is conceivably the most important sentiment of all. Regarding a woman who has been epithetically reduced to "homemaker," a single noun in the English language under the "head of the house," and concluding that she lacks profound importance, on par with that of her college years, is altogether unjust. The women of the early twentieth century helped build this country, within the limited visible authority they were afforded, in the home. Cecil may have been simplified, like so many other women, in the obscurities of tradition and societal structure, though regardless of her eventual position as an "every woman," viewing Cecil and her fellow coeds as new women during their years at Purdue lays the framework to understand them, not as a "types," but as *women*, full human beings. One may speculate with confidence that Cecil was a revolutionary under her own roof, maintaining a brilliant literary mind as a caring mother, an equal companion to her husband, and a community presence.

Bibliography

"The College World." *Exponent* (West Lafayette, IN), Feb. 18, 1904.

Crane, Cecil. "The Life and Works of George Sand." Senior thesis, Purdue University, 1904.

Debris. 1904. The Virginia Kelly Karnes Archives and Special Collections Research Center, Purdue University Libraries.

"Exchange Pages." *Exponent* (West Lafayette, IN), Dec. 3, 1903.

"Exchange Pages." *Exponent* (West Lafayette, IN), Mar. 3, 1904.

"Friendship." *Exponent* (West Lafayette, IN), Mar. 17, 1904.

Fuchs, Jeanne. "George Sand: Notorious Woman, Celebrated Writer," *The Coast of Utopia* 43 (2006): 1.

"A Gala Week." *Exponent* (West Lafayette, IN), Feb. 11, 1904.

"The Girl About the U." *Exponent* (West Lafayette, IN), Mar. 10, 1904.

"The Girls' Page." *Exponent* (West Lafayette, IN), Feb. 18, 1904.

Kasson, John. *Houdini, Tarzan, and the Perfect Man: The White Male Body and the Challenge of Modernity in America*. New York: Farrar, Straus and Giroux, 2002.

"Local Items." *Exponent* (West Lafayette, IN), Oct. 28, 1903.

Marcus, Sharon. Review "George Sand and Idealism" by Naomi Schor, *Comparative Literature* 109, no. 5 (1994): 1011.

"The Memorial Gymnasium." *Exponent* (West Lafayette, IN), Feb. 4, 1904.

"News." *Exponent* (West Lafayette, IN), Dec. 16, 1903.

"News." *Exponent* (West Lafayette, IN), Feb. 11, 1904.

"News." *Exponent* (West Lafayette, IN), Feb. 18, 1904.

"The Practical Religion of the College Girl." *Exponent* (West Lafayette, IN), Mar. 3, 1904.

Sivert, Eileen. "Lélia and Feminism." *Yale French Studies, Feminist Readings: French Texts/ American Contexts*, no. 62 (1981): 47.

"Strange Things Will Happen." *Exponent* (West Lafayette, IN), Feb. 11, 1904.

"The University." *Exponent* (West Lafayette, IN), Jan. 14, 1904.

Notes

1. John Kasson, *Houdini, Tarzan, and the Perfect Man: The White Male Body and the Challenge of Modernity in America* (New York: Farrar, Straus and Giroux, 2002), 13.

2. "Strange Things Will Happen," *Exponent* (West Lafayette, IN), Feb. 11, 1904.

3. *Debris*, 1904, the Virginia Kelly Karnes Archives and Special Collections Research Center, Purdue University Libraries, 247–48.

4. Ibid., 253.

5. Ibid., 75.

6. "Exchange Pages," *Exponent* (West Lafayette, IN), Mar. 3, 1904.

7. *Debris*, 1904, 254.

8. Ibid., 285.

9. "The College World," *Exponent* (West Lafayette, IN), Feb. 18, 1904.

10. "News," *Exponent* (West Lafayette, IN), Dec. 16, 1903.

11. "Local Items," *Exponent* (West Lafayette, IN), Oct. 28, 1903.

12. "Friendship," *Exponent* (West Lafayette, IN), Mar. 17, 1904.

13. "The Girl About the U," *Exponent* (West Lafayette, IN), Mar. 10, 1904.

14. "An Engineer's Idea of a Girl's Head," *Debris*, 1904, 301.

15. "The Memorial Gymnasium," *Exponent* (West Lafayette, IN), Feb. 4, 1904.

16. "News," *Exponent* (West Lafayette, IN), Feb. 11, 1904.

17. *Debris,* 1904, 75.

18. Ibid.

19. "Exchange Pages," *Exponent* (West Lafayette, IN), Dec. 3, 1903.

20. "The Practical Religion of the College Girl," *Exponent* (West Lafayette, IN), Mar. 3, 1904.

21. *Debris,* 1904, 196.

22. "News," *Exponent* (West Lafayette, IN), Feb. 18, 1904.

23. "A Gala Week," *Exponent* (West Lafayette, IN), Feb. 11, 1904.

24. Sharon Marcus, Review "George Sand and Idealism" by Naomi Schor, *Comparative Literature* 109, no. 5 (1994): 1011.

25. Jeanne Fuchs, "George Sand: Notorious Woman, Celebrated Writer," *The Coast of Utopia* 43 (2006): 1.

26. "The University," *Exponent* (West Lafayette, IN), Jan. 14, 1904.

27. Cecil Crane, "The Life and Works of George Sand" (senior thesis, Purdue University, 1904), 2.

28. Ibid., 3.

29. Ibid., 8.

30. Ibid., 10.

31. Ibid., 11. Purdue had its own, very different set of "devils." A group of male students known as the Dormitory Devils were responsible for terrorizing Purdue students at the turn of the century. It is possible that Crane was struck by the similar name in her research and the very different kind of group it represented for Sand versus the "boys'" culture at Purdue.

32. Ibid., 12.

33. Eileen Sivert, "Lélia and Feminism," *Yale French Studies, Feminist Readings: French Texts/ American Contexts*, no. 62 (1981): 47.

34. Ibid., 48.

35. Crane, "The Life and Works," 22–23.

36. Ibid., 22.

37. *Debris*, 1904, 247–48.

38. Ibid., 298.

39. Ibid., 132. Famed Purdue Alumnus George Ade wrote a play called *The College Widow* in 1904. After finding success on Broadway, it was made into a film, and was recently restaged here by the Purdue Theater Department.

40. Ibid., 75.

41. Ibid., 132.

42. "The Girls' Page," *Exponent* (West Lafayette, IN), Feb. 18, 1904.

The Lost Bandsman and His Band

 *Paige Zimmerman*

The Purdue "All-American" Marching Band. That is what "the best damn band in the land" is known as today. It is a band whose halftime performances celebrate everything from the veterans who have fought for our country to the pride of Purdue, but with a cinematic flair. This is what any student interested in auditioning to be a part of the "All-American" Marching Band in the twenty-first century can expect. But what about when the band first started? How has it changed since its founding in 1886?[1] What was it like in the early years of the twentieth century? These are exactly the kinds of questions that only a student from 1904 could answer. More specifically, these are questions that a bass drum player known as Frederic "Happy" Henry Miller could answer.

Unfortunately, not much was recorded during Frederic and his friends' time in the band. But it is time for this "lost" bandsman and his band to come out of the shadows. Perhaps by looking at the overall Purdue experience of that era, one can indirectly gain insight into the band.

Frederic was born around 1883 in Waynetown, Indiana. The son of Purdue alumnus J. N. Miller, he came to Purdue to study electrical engineering.[2] His friends called him by two nicknames: "The Prince" and "Happy."[3] While no description could be found about "The Prince," "Happy" Miller is described often. He had a smile that never left his face. One of the authors of the 1904 *Debris*, the student yearbook, recalled that he had "been able to partake of all the vices and virtues ordinarily allotted to the student without suffering in the least from either."[4] Students can suffer from dependence upon many different vices, such as pride or envy, but for each vice there is a virtue that can act as a counterforce. Virtues must be learned and nurtured. Living a virtuous life can be demanding, but it can be rewarding when reinforced.[5] That Frederic was able to partake in both and not suffer from either could mean that while he made a few poor choices, he was able to learn from them by practicing virtuous behavior more often than not. And while vices and virtues may have presented challenges, he emerged with rewarding results.

For his freshman, sophomore, and senior year, he played on the varsity football team. From his sophomore to senior year, he was a member of the Purdue Band. His senior year, he played the bass drum and was elected by his fellow bandsmen to the position of manager.[6]

In 1903, the band was entirely student-run, as it had been since its founding. There were no adult staff members; even the director was a student. At the turn

FIGURE 1. FREDERIC IS SEATED IN THE SECOND ROW WITH HIS HAND ON THE BASS DRUM (*DEBRIS* 1904, 180).

of the twentieth century, the band had grown from its original five volunteer members to thirty-five. Over time, new administrative positions were added to the organization, including president, secretary-treasurer, and manager.[7] A bandsman who was elected by the other members of the band filled each position. This meant that reorganization was frequent during the band's early years. The band did not have an official director until 1905.[8] Having student officers is not an uncommon tradition in bands today, but the idea of an entirely student-run college band is extraordinary.

The late 1800s to the turn of the twentieth century was an era when many individuals could not travel to concert halls for band performances. Given the natural human need and love for music, people entertained themselves by making music. As was common during this time, the formation of Purdue's band was inevitable. When the band began, it was known as the cadet drum corps.[9] The drum corps would play for the Purdue Student Army Training Corps during weekly drills.

As sports were introduced to the campus in the late 1800s, the band started to play at new events. By 1903, the group had officially become the "Purdue Band," performing at football and baseball games. The musical selections ranged from standard overtures to marches. In the late 1800s, John Philip Sousa was becoming famous all over the world for his marches.[10] It is plausible that a few of his pieces may have been included in the band's repertoire. The members of the band played at the games "without compensation for their services."[11] The research trails that were taken to gain some insight into what game days were like for the band and its involvement in the day have, more often than not, turned into dead ends.[12] The idea of what the members of the Purdue Band experienced on game days can only be imagined.

We do know, however, that as the band continued to grow and become a more prominent presence on campus, other members of Purdue University noticed. In 1900, the *Exponent*, a student-organized newspaper, praised the band, describing those who liked what they were seeing and hearing from these students: "Nothing tends more to develop in the students that keen sense of loyalty to Purdue than the band. Good college bands are such a rarity that the students in enumerating the many good things of Purdue are pleased to give this organization a prominent place on the list."[13]

The fact that playing in the band was entirely voluntary added to its charm, an aspect of the band that continues to this day. Every student who joined the band had his own instrument, and most of the musicians received musical education from friends and family. In those days, students did not have private lessons or band rehearsal during school. They would learn from their mothers and fathers, or they would walk to a neighbor down the street. Each student who joined the band at Purdue came because each wanted to continue with his love of music. All were independent musicians, but there existed "that unison and harmony which is necessary to the success of any musical organization."[14]

From the time Purdue first admitted students in 1874 until 1965, all male students were required to have two years of military training. Playing in the band would fulfill this requirement for students, as it was considered a military band.[15] The Purdue "All-American" Marching Band today still holds some traditions of being a military band in the way operations are conducted. Two examples are the inspection of uniforms before a performance and the receipt of rank titles as one logs more hours in the various offices. But while these traditions remain, there is no longer a military requirement of the students.

Fans and historians of the Purdue football program may be familiar with the fateful day of October 31, 1903, which has also become known as the day of the "Purdue Wreck." What might be forgotten, however, was that the band was there too. Frederic and his teammates had boarded a train that was to take them to face Indiana University in a football game the morning of October 31. The football team and a few special guests rode as passengers in the first car, followed by the band, a few professors, and other guests in the second car.[16] The rest of the cars were filled with people attending the game. Spectators, who were to board a later train, came to cheer the team on as the first train pulled out of the station.

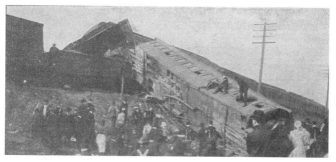

FIGURE 2. THE PURDUE WRECK (*DEBRIS* 1904, 22).

At 9:45 a.m., the train was nearing Indianapolis. The train followed the curve of the tracks, just as a ten-section group of coal cars approached from the opposite direction. The two trains collided, and the wooden car carrying the football team was crushed.

The second car containing the band came off the tracks and slid down into a gravel pit. Although the seats came loose and the passengers fell to the back of the car, no one in the band was seriously injured or killed. All of those who were able worked to get everyone out of the car. One of Frederic's fellow bandsmen gave an account of what went on to the *Lafayette Courier:* "We had to pass seats out of the windows so that we could get out. . . . I don't know just how we got out, but we climbed through the windows, I remember, because the door couldn't be reached. . . . Not one of the band members were injured, but some of us lost our coats and instruments. . . . We got them [the girls who were passengers] away from there as fast as we could."[17]

The total number of deaths from this tragic accident was seventeen. More than forty were seriously injured. Thirteen of the losses were members of the football team, with twenty-nine other members hospitalized.[18] Frederic received an injury to his head, and like his other teammates who weren't severely injured, he went home to recover.[19] He returned to campus one week later.[20] By then, discussion was taking place regarding a way to memorialize and honor those who had lost their lives. This resulted in the decision to build the Memorial Gymnasium, which still stands on campus today under the name Hass Hall. Ground was broken four years after Frederic's graduation, and the dedication took place on May 19, 1909.[21] It was said that the Purdue Wreck was the only time "the smile was wiped from" "Happy" Miller's face.[22]

Frederic graduated with his class in the spring of 1904. After graduation, he went to Crawfordsville, Indiana, where he was in charge of an electrical plant for about six months. He then went to Versailles, Ohio, and after that to Arcanum, Ohio. In both cities, Frederic was in charge of a light and heat plant. In 1905, he married a woman named Gertrude Melvina Beare.[23] They had two children: a daughter named Martha and a son named Frederic, Jr., who followed his father's footsteps by studying at Purdue.

By 1914, Frederic had returned to Indiana. He was appointed as superintendent of the Crawfordsville Municipal Electric Light Plant.[24] He retained his ties with Purdue by becoming the secretary of the 1904 class.[25] While he personally didn't have any entries in the Purdue *Alumnus* after 1914, he was included in an article about his son in 1943.[26] From that point on, his archival trail runs dry. Frederic did not live what some may consider an exciting life, but that does not make his time at Purdue any less important. He was one of the survivors of the 1903 tragedy, and he contributed to the early years of the Purdue Band.

Everyone who has participated in the program over the years has impacted the organization. This continues to be the case with the Purdue bands. Students devote their time and energy purely for the love of music, resulting in an extraordinary program even without a formal college of music, carrying on a tradition from the earliest days of the band.

There has not been much written about what being in the band would have been like for Frederic and his fellow bandsmen; however, hopefully an outsider looking in to this time from Frederic's perspective could glimpse what it might have been like, helping one to better understand how the Purdue "All-American" Marching Band became what it is today.

Bibliography

1910 Census, Toledo Ward 8, Lucas, Ohio; Roll: T624_1209; Page: 7B; Enumeration District: 0101; FHL microfilm: 1375222; citing National Archives and Records Administration microfilm publication T624, roll 1209. *Ancestry.com. A*ccessed November 17, 2013. http://www.ancestry.com.

"Character: Virtue vs. Vice." Southern Connecticut State University. Accessed January 30, 2013. http://home.southernct.edu/~cassoj2/character.htm.

Lindquist, Danille Christensen. "'Locating' the Nation: Football Game Day and American Dreams in Central Ohio." *Journal of American Folklore* 119, no. 474 (Fall 2006): 448–88.

Norberg, John. *Heartbeat of the University: 125 Years of Purdue Bands*. West Lafayette, IN: Purdue University Press, 2011.

Purdue *Alumnus*. 1914. The Virginia Kelly Karnes Archives and Special Collections Research Center, Purdue University Libraries.

———. 1943. The Virginia Kelly Karnes Archives and Special Collections Research Center, Purdue University Libraries.

Purdue *Debris*. 1904. The Virginia Kelly Karnes Archives and Special Collections Research Center, Purdue University Libraries.

Purdue *Exponent* (West Lafayette, IN), 1903.

Notes

1. John Norberg, *Heartbeat of the University: 125 Years of Purdue Bands* (West Lafayette, IN: Purdue University, 2011).

2. *Alumnus*, 1914, the Virginia Kelly Karnes Archives and Special Collections Research Center, Purdue University Libraries.

3. *Debris*, 1904, the Virginia Kelly Karnes Archives and Special Collections Research Center, Purdue University Libraries, 98.

4. Ibid.

5. "Character: Virtue vs. Vice," Southern Connecticut State University, accessed January 30, 2013, http://home.southernct.edu/~cassoj2/character.htm.

6. *Debris*, 1904.

7. Norberg, 2011.

8. "Purdue University Bands: Celebrating 125 Years," *Hall of Music Productions*, 2011.

9. Norberg, 2011.

10. Ibid., 4.

11. Ibid., 6.

12. While there are a few articles that have been written about other bands in the early twentieth century, such as *The Pride of the Buckeyes: The Ohio State University Marching Band*, there is very little to be found about the Purdue Band. For further information about Big Ten school football teams and marching bands, see Danille Christensen Lindquist, "'Locating' the Nation: Football Game Day and American Dreams in Central Ohio," *Journal of American Folklore* 119, no. 474 (Fall 2006).

13. Norberg, 2011.

14. Ibid., 6.

15. Ibid., 6.

16. "Purdue University Bands: Celebrating 125 Years," 2011, http://www.purdue.edu/bands/merchandise/Band%20125%20DVD.pdf.

17. Norberg, 2011.

18. Ibid., 9.

19. *Exponent* (West Lafayette, IN), 1903.

20. Ibid.

21. Norberg, 2011.

22. *Debris*, 1904.

23. *Ancestery.com*, Year: 1910; Census Place: Toledo Ward 8, Lucas, Ohio; Roll: T624_1209; Page: 7B; Enumeration District: 0101; FHL microfilm: 1375222., 2013.

24. *Alumnus*, 1914.

25. *Alumnus*, 1943, the Virginia Kelly Karnes Archives and Special Collections Research Center, Purdue University Libraries.

26. Ibid. For further information about Frederic Henry Miller, Jr., see "Boilermaker Assumes Key Role."

Just Harry

Lily Anderson

Harry Leon Hodges was an ordinary man in an extraordinary situation. The average eighteen-year-old male in the early 1900s had very few options open to him. Generally, he was expected to take over the family business or find a job as a nameless face in the workforce. Many men like Harry would find themselves working in factories and shops, or performing manual labor. These men would do their best to scrape together a living, with little time for frivolities or new experiences.[1] Harry broke this mold.

When Harry first attended Purdue University in 1898,[2] only 2 percent of eighteen to twenty-four-year-olds in the United States were enrolled at a higher education institution.[3] With such a small percentage attending college, one would expect stories of geniuses, of beating the odds, and of exceptionalism. That is not Harry's story.

Harry did not come from the slums and work his way up; he came from an average family and lived in West Lafayette, Indiana. Harry did not attend Purdue and become the big man on campus; he attended and quietly obtained a standard education. Harry did not leave Purdue and revolutionize the field of civil engineering; he went on to work and support a family. He was a man to which many can relate. He was just Harry, and sometimes, that is the story most worth telling.[4]

Our heroes define us. They cause the small child to put on a cape and the mature adult to hang his up. Harry's own hero was not perfect, but he was a man who made his own way in life, worked hard, and survived trials. Harry's life often mirrored the life of his hero, sometimes by following in his footsteps, other times by sidestepping his mistakes. His hero was an average man, but as is often the case with heroes, Harry saw someone much more than average. Harry saw a man worth looking up to. Harry saw his father, Everett Macy Hodges.

Everett's life began like that of most average men: he was born. This man in particular, however, was born in rural New York to a successful farmer with many sons.[5] As was often the case in that time, the farm did not pass to the middle child, Everett, but rather to an older sibling.[6] This is perhaps why, in 1880, Everett came to work in Indiana as a dry goods clerk.[7]

It was a less than glamorous position. An 1864 *New York Times* article sums up the general situation for dry goods clerks: "There are hundreds of young men in this city eking out miserable lives as clerks, without the shadow of a chance of their ever being better off."[8] Everett toiled away as one of those clerks for over twenty years, in the same place he first started. Through no real fault of his own, his career was stagnant, with no ladder to climb or even fall off of. However, that does not necessarily mean Everett was unhappy; his work was steady and allowed him to raise and support a family. His life may not have been exciting, but his hardworking nature allowed his children to grow up in a stable environment in a period when such things were often uncertain.

Sadly though, Everett's life was not without trials. When Everett was still just a farmer's son living in the state of New York, he had wooed a young girl away from the big city of Manhattan, and together, Everett and

Jennie Hodges left New York for the Midwest. Far away from friends, family, and familiarity,[9] they made West Lafayette, Indiana, their home.[10] Their first child was born shortly after they were married, a little boy named Everett Vinnedge.[11] It was a harsh time to be young and vulnerable,[12] however, and after only one year, Everett and Jennie buried their firstborn son.[13] They persevered though, and went on to have four more children,[14] including Harry.[15] For thirty-seven years they were partners through every trouble and triumph. When Jennie died in 1912, Everett lost something crucial.[16] Shortly after Jennie's passing,[17] Everett left Indiana to live with his oldest child in Tennessee and did not return until 1920, when he was buried and reunited at last with her and their infant son.[18]

Everett never wore a cape, but that did not matter; he was not the world's hero, just Harry's. However, Harry was not his father. Everett gave Harry the chance to be something greater. The farmer's son became a clerk, and the clerk's son became an engineer. Perhaps more importantly though, when many were growing up too soon, Everett gave Harry the chance to be a kid and fully enjoy what the world had to offer before plunging into the trials and tribulations of adult life. Harry received a cape of gold and black and the honor of becoming a Purdue man, including all of the experiences and traditions that came with such a title.[19]

Dorm Devils cackled, mechanical textbooks crackled, and tank scrappers tackled.[20] Purdue was in no way a boring place in the early 1900s, and Harry found himself in the middle of a living, breathing campus full of culture and opportunities. It would be nigh impossible to attend and not have at least a little Purdue spirit rub off. Harry watched as the Dorm Devils, dressed up in white with pitchforks, hazed and terrorized startled freshmen. He stood solemnly with the other seniors as they rid themselves of their loathed mechanical textbooks in a ritualistic burning ceremony. If he wanted to count himself as a true Purdue man, he definitely defended his class's honor at the ol' Tank Scrap, knocking out a few teeth.[21] Harry enjoyed sports, playing on the class football team as quarterback and serving as captain,[22] as well as competing successfully in wrestling tournaments.[23] I am sure he attended at least one convocation, perhaps even sitting in the front row as James Whitcomb Riley entertained the Purdue student body.[24] If one became bored with the numerous extracurricular activities offered on campus, there also was rigorous class work. Make no mistake, even though the members of the class of 1904 were born over one hundred years ago, they were not that different from Purdue students today, as evidenced by this student's poem published in a 1903 *Exponent*:

> There be phrases that please for their very words.
> And some that do good on occasion
> There be some that are used by the girl back home,
> And some of parental dictation
> But of all that I know, from please keep enclosed to
> "Fall in with no guns and sidearms" there is one that
> surpasses all other in weight,
> To one which the coldest of hearts warms
> When the calculus prof. with cold glances entrenched
> Says surly, losing his prey,
> "Owing to the class' misunderstanding, there will be
> no test today."[25]

Also like students today, no matter how much they grumbled, they were expected to hold their own academically. For his degree in civil engineering, Harry was taught to master the skills of forging, mechanical drawing, physics, topography, calculus, chemistry, hydraulics, wood working, molding, surveying, and studies of materials and structure. He also needed to learn the basics of history, writing, German, and rudimentary mathematics.[26] Getting into Purdue was not necessarily difficult, but staying there could be a struggle.

Purdue tuition in the early 1900s was either free or very cheap for most students,[27] and being a land-grant college, Purdue's goal was to educate as many as possible rather than create a reputation of exclusivity.[28] For Harry, a young man living within walking distance of campus with no career lined up, Purdue may have seemed an easy choice, and becoming a Boilermaker meant Harry would experience a level of education and culture that few others could even imagine.[29] However, Harry did not know this at the time. When offered a job that would put money in his pocket immediately compared to two more years of calculus in pursuit of an uncertain career, walking away from Purdue made sense. Harry had no idea of the trials to come and how much those memories would mean to him; thus, like many other students, Harry dropped out.[30]

Students left Purdue for a variety of reasons—most for the same reason as those who never enrolled in the first place. At the turn of the century, a college education was not particularly valuable. Things were starting to change, but most employers were still more interested in hands-on experience rather than theoretical knowledge.[31] This way of thinking explains how Harry was able to easily get a job working for the local railroad. For two years he worked at the Big Four Railroad Company. Harry likely could have remained there for as long as he wanted, and no one would have batted an eye if he never returned to Purdue. However, Harry chose a different path, and in 1902, he reenrolled at Purdue to complete his education.

Sometimes having someone you look up to also means avoiding their pitfalls. Whether Harry was taking his father's advice or acting on his own observation does not matter; the result was the same. Harry did not take the first job that came along, but rather, he started on a road his father never could have hoped to walk down. Harry "The Kid" Hodges[32] was privileged to have had a chance to develop and enjoy himself away from the working world, but when it came time to plunge back in, he was ready. He hung up his cape, picked up a hammer, and started his adult life as a Purdue Boilermaker.

Harry's working life began like that of most average men: he got a job. This job in particular, though, was for the railroad. In 1906, Harry was hard at work on the Oregon Short Line in Mill City, Nevada. His adult life started off much like his father's life did: a young man far from home, trying to find his place. Also like his father, he was not alone in his journey.[33] He too brought a girl from home with him, and on June 19, 1907, Harry married Elizabeth Miles of Indiana.[34]

Harry and Elizabeth followed the train tracks, and when it came time to start a family in 1909, Harry was working for a railroad company in Utah. Harry and his wife had a much happier start to their family than his father, and little William Everett was alive and well when his sister, Helen Elizabeth, joined them in 1911. Together, the small family moved from place to place, following the railroads.[35] The work was not always easy, but it was a booming industry and good place to be an engineer in the early 1900s.[36] Unfortunately, darker days were ahead.

On October 29, 1929, the stock market crashed, and over fifteen million Americans were suddenly without jobs. Harry, while trying to raise and support a family, found himself in the midst of the Great Depression. With suicide and unemployment rates rising significantly, no one would have been surprised if Harry had given up.[37] However, Harry Hodges was not that kind of man. At times he found himself working entry-level positions, but Harry pressed on. Despite the bleak situation, he worked his way up from a draftsman in Utah[38] to an engineer for the Indiana Department of Transportation in Indianapolis.[39] In a period when many were barely scraping by, Harry fought to take the situation he was given and make it better.

When Harry died in 1955, he left behind the story of a dependable, adaptable, and practical man. An unassuming headstone marks his final resting place at Crown Hill Cemetery in Indianapolis, fifty-two miles from where he started.[40] He lived in extraordinary times and situations, but he himself was never an out-of-the-ordinary man. Sometimes, though, it is the people who lived history whom we need to hear from more than those who made it.

I would like to think Harry kept his 1900 class motto in mind as he made his way in the world: "Within Thine Own Sphere, Accomplish What Thou Canst."[41] His life was not a story of tragedy, achievement, or heroism; it was just a story of day-to-day struggles. He looked up to his father and tried to make him proud, but he also tried to surpass his father's accomplishments. His choice to attend Purdue did not drastically change his life, but it set him apart and gave him experiences few others could claim. He fought to stay afloat in a time when many sunk, and he left behind a well-cared-for family. Most of all, he worked to lead the best life he could with the options available to him. He will not be found in any famous stories, but he will be found here. Most of us do not live a life for the history books, and neither did he. He was just Harry, and that is just fine.

Bibliography

"America at Work, America at Leisure." *Library of Congress*. Accessed November 25, 2013. http://memory.loc.gov/ammem/awlhtml/awlhome.html.

Anderson, Ryan K. "'The Law of College Customs is [as] Inexorable as the Laws of Chemistry or Physics':

The Transition to a Modern Purdue University, 1900–1924." *Indiana Magazine of History* (June 2003): 97–128.

The Annual Catalogue of Purdue University, 1902–1903. The Virginia Kelly Karnes Archives and Special Collections Research Center, Purdue University Libraries.

"An Appeal to Dry-Goods Clerks." *New York Times* (January 24, 1864). Accessed November 13, 2013. http://www.nytimes.com/1864/01/24/news/an-appeal-to-dry-goods-clerks.html.

The Bureau of the Census. *Eighth Census of the United States, 1860.* Washington, DC: Records of the Bureau of the Census, 1860.

———. *Tenth Census of the United States, 1880.* Washington, DC: Records of the Bureau of the Census, 1880.

———. *Twelfth Census of the United States, 1900.* Washington, DC: Records of the Bureau of the Census, 1900.

———. *Fourteenth Census of the United States, 1920.* Washington, DC: Records of the Bureau of the Census, 1920.

"Everett Macy Hodges." *Find a Grave.* Accessed November 25, 2013. http://www.findagrave.com/cgi-bin/fg.cgi?page=gr&GSln=HOD&GSpartial

=1&GSbyrel=all&GSst=17&GScntry=4&GSsr=1001&GRid=92060215&.

"The Great Depression." *PBS*. Accessed November 25, 2013. http://www.pbs.org/wgbh/americanexperience/features/general-article/dustbowl-great-depression.

"Harry Leon Hodges." *Find a Grave*. Accessed November 25, 2013. http://www.findagrave.com/cgi-bin/fg.cgi?page=gr&GSln=HOD&GSpartial=1&GSbyrel=all&GSst=17&GScntry=4&GSsr=1081&GRid=45947652&.

Heslop, Madison. "Murky Drops from Old Pump Rotten: The Old Pump, the 'Purdue Woman,' and the Ancient Order of the Dormitory Devils." *Journal of Purdue Undergraduate Research* 3 (2013): 44–49. http://dx.doi.org/10.5703/jpur.03.14.07.

"Infant Mortality and Life Expectancy." *PBS*. Accessed November 25, 2013. http://www.pbs.org/fmc/timeline/dmortality.htm.

National Center for Education Statistics. *120 Years of American Education: A Statistical Portrait,* Edited by Thomas D. Snyder. N.P.: US Department of Education, 1993.

Purdue *Alumnus*. 1914. The Virginia Kelly Karnes Archives and Special Collections Research Center, Purdue University Libraries.

Purdue *Debris*. 1899. The Virginia Kelly Karnes Archives and Special Collections Research Center, Purdue University Libraries.

———. 1900. The Virginia Kelly Karnes Archives and Special Collections Research Center, Purdue University Libraries.

———. 1904. The Virginia Kelly Karnes Archives and Special Collections Research Center, Purdue University Libraries.

Purdue University Alumni Directory, 1875–1934. 1934. The Virginia Kelly Karnes Archives and Special Collections Research Center, Purdue University Libraries.

Purdue University Register of Alumni, 1875–1906. 1906. The Virginia Kelly Karnes Archives and Special Collections Research Center, Purdue University Libraries.

———, *1875–1911*. 1912. The Virginia Kelly Karnes Archives and Special Collections Research Center, Purdue University Libraries.

Rodenberger, Joan. "Newspaper Index, 1902–1952." 2003. *Lafayette Journal and Courier*.

T. D. S. "And This Best of All." *Exponent* (West Lafayette, IN), 1903.

Thale, Christopher. "Railroad Workers." *Encyclopedia of Chicago*. Accessed November 25, 2013. http://

www.encyclopedia.chicagohistory.org/pages/1038.html.

Thelin, John R., Jason R. Edwards, and Eric Moyen. "Higher Education in the United States—Historical Development, System." *Education Encyclopedia*. Accessed November 25, 2013. http://education.stateuniversity.com/pages/2044/Higher-Education-in-United-States.html.

"The Visit of the Hoosier Poet." *Exponent* (West Lafayette, IN), 1903.

Notes

1. "America at Work and Leisure," *Library of Congress*, accessed November 25, 2013, http://memory.loc.gov/ammem/awlhtml/awlhome.html.

2. *Debris*, 1904, the Virginia Kelly Karnes Archives and Special Collections Research Center, Purdue University Libraries, 86.

3. National Center for Education Statistics, *120 Years of American Education: A Statistical Portrait*, ed. Thomas D. Snyder (n.p.: US Department of Education, 1993), 76.

4. *Debris*, 1904, 86.

5. The Bureau of the Census, *Eighth Census of the United States* (Washington, DC: Records of the Bureau of the Census, 1860), 445.

6. John R. Thelin, Jason R. Edwards, and Eric Moyen, "Higher Education in the United States—Historical Development, System," *Education Encyclopedia*, accessed November 25, 2013, http://education.stateuniversity.com/pages/2044/Higher-Education-in-United-States.html.

7. The Bureau of the Census, *Tenth Census of the United States* (Washington, DC: Records of the Bureau of the Census, 1880), 338B.

8. "An Appeal to Dry-Goods Clerks," *New York Times* (January 24, 1864), accessed November 13, 2013, http://www.nytimes.com/1864/01/24/news/an-appeal-to-dry-goods-clerks.html.

9. The Bureau of the Census, *Eighth Census of the United States*, 445.

10. The Bureau of the Census, *Tenth Census of the United States*, 338B.

11. "Everett Macy Hodges," *Find a Grave*, accessed November 25, 2013, http://www.findagrave.com/cgibin/fg.cgi?page=gr&GSln=HOD&GSpartial=1&GSbyrel=all&GSst=17&Scntry=4&GSsr=1001&GRid=92060215&.

12. "Infant Mortality and Life Expectancy," *PBS*, accessed November 25, 2013, http://www.pbs.org/fmc/timeline/dmortality.htm.

13. "Everett Macy Hodges," *Find a Grave*.

14. The Bureau of the Census, *Twelfth Census of the United States* (Washington, DC: Records of the Bureau of the Census, 1900), 8B.

15. The Bureau of the Census, *Tenth Census of the United States*, 338B.

16. "Everett Macy Hodges," *Find a Grave*.

17. Ibid.

18. The Bureau of the Census, *Fourteenth Census of the United States* (Washington, DC: Records of the Bureau of the Census, 1920), 3A.

19. *Debris*, 1904, 86.

20. Refer to the introduction of this book for more information. The Dorm Devils were a hazing group on campus. The Mechanics Burning was a popular event at Purdue, where seniors would destroy their mechanical textbooks at the end of the year. Tank Scrap referred to an annual event in which the incoming freshman class would physically fight the sophomore class for painting rights on the water tower. See Madison

Heslop's "Murky Drops" for a discussion of the Dorm Devils and gender at Purdue.

21. Ryan K. Anderson, "The Law of College Customs is [as] Inexorable as the Laws of Chemistry or Physics": The Transition to a Modern Purdue University, 1900–1924," *Indiana Magazine of History* (June 2003): 97–128, 104, 110–14.

22. *Debris*, 1899, the Virginia Kelly Karnes Archives and Special Collections Research Center, Purdue University Libraries, 117.

23. *Debris*, 1900, the Virginia Kelly Karnes Archives and Special Collections Research Center, Purdue University Libraries, 116.

24. "The Visit of the Hoosier Poet," *Exponent* (West Lafayette, IN), 1903, 5.

25. T. D. S., "And This Best of All," *Exponent* (West Lafayette, IN), 1903, 6.

26. *The Annual Catalogue of Purdue University, 1902–1903*, the Virginia Kelly Karnes Archives and Special Collections Research Center, Purdue University Libraries, 84–95.

27. Anderson, 99–100.

28. *The Annual Catalogue of Purdue University, 1902–1903*, 169–79.

29. Ibid., 197.

30. *Debris*, 1904, 86, 120–21.

31. Purdue *Alumnus*, 1914, the Virginia Kelly Karnes Archives and Special Collections Research Center, Purdue University Libraries, 25.

32. *Debris*, 1904, 86.

33. *Purdue University Register of Alumni, 1875–1906*, 1906, the Virginia Kelly Karnes Archives and Special Collections Research Center, Purdue University Libraries, 49.

34. Joan Rodenberger, "*Newspaper Index, 1902–1952,*" 2003, *Lafayette Journal and Courier.*

35. The Bureau of the Census, *Fourteenth Census of the United States,* 12A.

36. Christopher Thale, "Railroad Workers," Encyclopedia of Chicago, accessed November 25, 2013, http://www.encyclopedia.chicagohistory.org/pages/1038.html.

37. "The Great Depression," *PBS,* accessed November 25, 2013, http://www.pbs.org/wgbh/americanexperience/features/general-article/dustbowl-great-depression.

38. *Purdue University Register of Alumni, 1875–1911,* 1912, the Virginia Kelly Karnes Archives and Special Collections Research Center, Purdue University Libraries, 34.

39. *Purdue University Alumni Directory, 1875-1934,* 1934, the Virginia Kelly Karnes Archives and Special Collections Research Center, Purdue University Libraries, 274.

40. "Harry Leon Hodges," *Find a Grave,* accessed November 25, 2013, http://www.findagrave.com/cgibin/fg.cgi?page=gr&GSln=HOD&GSpartial=1&GSbyrel=all&GSst=17&GScntry=4&GSsr=1081&GRid=45947652&,.

41. *Debris,* 1900, 101.

Epilogue: Purdue's Past through Purdue's Present

Susan Curtis

THE ESSAYS THAT comprise *Little Else Than a Memory* show what can happen when students learn how to discover the complexity of history by finding people like themselves in the archives. History, with a capital "H," too often connotes epic battles, heroic leaders, world-shifting events, and grand narratives of the rising and falling of the fortunes of human beings. But packed in the ten essays you have just read are historical sketches and analyses that help readers, and I daresay the authors, make sense of a critically important aspect of modern life—attending college and earning a baccalaureate degree. In the course of looking for members of the class of 1904, these student authors have discovered that it is impossible to write the history of these individuals or of the university they attended without also appreciating the larger context of the world they inhabited.

Purdue University in 1904 was an institution shaped by and implicated in the process of modernization. In that year, the United States was just beginning to creep out of a decade-long depression that had left thousands of Americans jobless and homeless, had placed constraints on the life chances of millions of Americans, and culminated in an affirmation of an urban, industrial, and technological future for the nation and the world. As a land-grant university, founded under the auspices of the 1862 Morrill Act, Purdue in 1904 was a thirty-five-year-old institution known for its courses of study in engineering and agriculture. Even then, it played an important role in preparing students for professional careers in fields that would lead the United States away from its small-town, agrarian past. The tragedy of that academic year—the train wreck on October 31, 1903, in Indianapolis, carrying students, faculty, and Purdue supporters to a football game against Indiana University—provided the leaders of the University an opportunity to ponder what its mission was to be in the future. With the inspiring words of President Winthrop Stone, faculty and students in the coming years embraced the goal of gaining control over the forces of nature through engineering and science—theirs was a noble aspiration to use scientific knowledge and expertise for the betterment of humankind.

Of course, students who flocked to campus in the early 1900s came for many other reasons as well. These essays offer readers a glimpse of the variety of reasons. Students from other countries came to the United States to obtain an education at a new, vibrant land-grant institution. Women and African Americans sought an education that up to that time was not always made available to them. Children of immigrants hoped that a credential from an American university would help them achieve the dream of upward mobility as well as acceptance as Americans. Once enrolled, students joined clubs, played in the band, took part in pranks, and expressed their ideas in the *Exponent,* orations, *Debris* entries, and rituals like the lynching of the mechanic. In one important sense, they were, in 1904, very much like the students who wrote about them—busy preparing for adulthood, establishing lifetime friendships, and trying to "find themselves" during a four-year hiatus from the demands of the workaday world.

In every one of these essays we learn something about how that four (or more) years of self-discovery affected individuals. From the opening essay about the two Henry Satterfields, we can see explicitly what was at stake in 1904 to have a college degree. Two boys with the same name from the same hometown ended up with very different life stories. The chief difference may well have been that one of those Henry Satterfields held a baccalaureate degree from Purdue. We find Joseph Burke Knapp adapting his degree in engineering to fit the needs of the food-shipping industry, which relied heavily on wood products. Joseph had obviously learned more than "the right answers" to test questions in engineering; he had learned how to approach problems and find solutions through critical, creative thinking. His Box-Shook method of shipping foodstuffs helped the US provide food safely to troops during World War I, a feat that had eluded the nation during its war with Spain in 1898, when many soldiers died from tainted beef. The volume ends with Harry Hodges, a dropout who eventually returned to the University after a few years of work. "Just Harry," as the author calls him, discovered that a college degree, despite how well or poorly he performed in individual classes, opened doors that simply were not available to those without the degree—those, like his father,

Everett Hodges, who plugged away in dead-end jobs in order to make a university education possible for their children. The essays in this volume offer a timely reminder of the many ways that a university education can affect the person who attains it; perhaps the most important result is that of providing undergraduates with more and better tools for making sense of the world in which they live. They learn how to demystify the unknown instead of fearing it.

One of the essays gives readers a glimpse of what run-of-the-mill white, native-born male students might have expected to experience as Boilermakers in 1904. Henry Miller joined the band, whose origins lie in the military training expected at land-grant universities. Miller, like many "All-American" band members before and after his day, did not become a professional musician, but being in the band was an integral part of his experience and sheds light on a fact that not everyone remembers—namely, all male students were expected to undergo military training for at least two years while enrolled at the University.

The essays devoted to Lyla Marshall Harcoff and Cecil Clare Crane open a window onto the lives of female students growing up in the heyday of the "New Woman." Unlike her demure, home-oriented foremother, the New Woman dared—dared to study at a male-dominated university, dared to study art instead of one of the sciences, dared to poke fun at her classmates, and dared to seek a credential that would allow her to enjoy professional opportunities and personal autonomy. Their stories remind us of the long struggle for equality in which women have engaged for more than a century. Like the men with whom they shared classrooms, these women used their experience at Purdue to arm themselves with an arsenal of analytical tools that they employed to make space for pioneering female professionals. Like Cecil, they considered the radical possibilities that women like George Sand advanced. Although Purdue was dominated by men in 1904, women like Lyla and Cecil made themselves felt in the daily life of students on campus; they left palpable traces of what it meant to be a woman at the dawn of the twentieth century seeking a baccalaureate degree.

In a similar vein, Robert Wirt Smith's story is a valuable reminder of the opportunities that awaited African American graduates of a land-grant university. Robert's degree in pharmacy gave him the credential to open a drug store in the vibrant early 1900s African American community in Indianapolis. The essay that showcases his presence at Purdue and his success afterward also demonstrates how research in one venue can lead readily to another. In order to track

Robert, the author had to read the African American newspapers of Indianapolis—and in the process, she found him in the midst of what W. E. B. Du Bois called the "talented tenth." Robert was a professional and was married to an educator. He would have offered young black children in Indianapolis a role model for upward mobility through classical education, not manual training. Likewise, the "Windy City Boys," Emil Farkas and William Raymond Davis, as well as Hugo Berthold and Sukichi Yoshisaka, all represent "outsiders"—men not from the same native-born, small-town, rural American world of the vast majority of Boilermakers in 1904. None of them quite fit in, and they were, for the most part, more difficult to track after they left West Lafayette. But their presence speaks to the growing reputation of Purdue University in the early twentieth century as well as to its incipient international flavor.

In writing about who fit in and who did not, the authors of these essays rely heavily on student-generated publications in the early twentieth century. Their reading of these materials sometimes exposes a world of difference between the undergraduate experience of the early 1900s and that of today. It needs to be emphasized that the entire student population in 1904 was around 1,440. Anyone who has lived in a community of that size knows that it is possible to know everyone to one degree or another. Because of their intimacy and visibility, students engaged in a discourse that is not entirely familiar on today's campus that is home to 38,000 students. The members of the class of 1904 took jabs at one another—playfully, most of the time. They exaggerated individual traits for humorous effect. But mostly, they were able to describe one another because they *knew* one another. They took part in sports, literary societies, clubs, and classwork side by side. They found ways to situate people who were different from themselves, whether that difference stemmed from ethnicity, race, gender, or childhood home. The comments students made about one another that might seem disparaging might better be seen as evidence of a double-edged humor—disparaging, to be sure, but based on actual knowledge of and perhaps affection for one another.

The authors of these essays are to be commended for delving into the unfamiliar world of the turn of the twentieth century and finding ways to make meaning out of their experience as "time travelers." Perhaps unwittingly, their essays also shed light on their own experience as Purdue University undergraduate students. Most good historical writing does so. Historians choose subjects for their research that are meaningful to them or that they believe can help their readers better comprehend the world around them. So it is not surprising that we learn something about Purdue students in the present by reading what they have written about Purdue students from more than a century ago. Because the student body of 2014 is diverse in terms of gender, race, and nativity, students showed interest in finding out what the experience was like for those groups in the past. Today, Purdue University takes pride in being a "global" university and home to the second largest number of international students in a US public university. That reality of today is reflected in the student authors' interest in the international students of 1904.

Perhaps as important as the choice of subjects is what the biographies communicate about today's students' aspirations for themselves. Their narratives looked for evidence of "fitting in" and "belonging" to the Purdue community. They longed to see evidence of their subjects' presence on campus as more than people attending lectures, taking exams, and getting grades. They reported on the organizations to which they belonged and rued the fact if they belonged to none; they looked for them in the student newspaper and in the *Debris*. Most of all, they showcased the way that getting an education affected the life chances of their subjects. Their beautifully written, well-researched essays are evidence of the power of the learning experience available at universities like Purdue—learning experiences that challenge students to head into the unknown and to return with their own hard-won truths.

Biographical Subject and Author Cameos from, and in the Style of, the *Debris* 1904–2014

Howard Ernest Satterfield, B. S. in Mechanical Engineering. Tau Beta Pi; Masonic Club; Y . M. C. A., President (4). Thesis: Investigations as to the Designs and Holding Powers of Transmission Blocks as Applied to Conveying Cables. Howard comes from the thriving town of Fairmount in the great State of West Virginia. He learned his A B C's at Fairmount State Normal. Howard couldn't be called a ranter, he is too quiet, but in the matter of hustling after knowledge he has shown many a clean pair of heels. His favorite girl's name is Grace, though we do not know why. He is bound to make a success because he is such a patient, hard worker.

Eden Bethany Holmes entered the world with words already on her tongue, and she hasn't stopped talking since. Emerging from the wilds of Tennessee, she was drawn to Purdue University as the characteristic black and gold colors brought out her eyes. She can never come up with enough to do in West Lafayette, with the enumeration of different extracurricular activities taking all her fingers (and a few toes) to count off. Like the famous detective who shares her surname, "Sherlock" aspires to turn her quick wit and passion for the truth to a career in criminal justice. As the queen of argument, Eden's fast mouth has drawn her to a future in a legal field.

Richard Wirt Smith, Graduate in Pharmacy. Smith is somewhat of a "Buttinsky," but it is partly excusable, as he is the only one of his kind in the Pharmacy Class. He is the best baseball player in the class and has had considerable experience along that line, having caught for the Manual Training School before entering Purdue. He has made a good record in his studies and has also been busy on the East Side, as it is there that he is called "Spoony." He is from Indianapolis.

Maggie Suzanne Mace is a very intelligent young woman who is striving to be in the FBI one day. She is a junior who majors in Law and Society with minors in Forensic Science and Psychology. She is also in the Honors College of Liberal Arts. She is the president of the Forensic Science Club and also serves as the president of Alpha Kappa Delta (an honors sociological society). She is a member of the sorority Alpha Omicron Pi. She has made a very good record here at Purdue University with all of her involvement and success. She is from Fishers, Indiana.

EMIL FARKAS, B. S. in Civil Engineering. Thesis: A Tunnel Under the Chicago River. "Fuzzy" rolled down here from Armour Institute last fall, wearing his expansive smile, and proceeded to make himself at home in the Civil department. He got credit for nearly all of his Armour work, but just to show him that Armour is nowhere in it with Purdue, a certain individual known as "Pansy" let him complete Theory of Structures and Mechanics and then made him take Junior Stresses. "King Dodo" is never so delighted as when he can find some one to listen to his fairy stories of how they do it up at Armour. He has an innocent, babyish face, which coupled with his enthusiastic gabble completely disarms us all, and we can't help liking him. Of course he comes from Chicago.

William Raymond Davis, B. S. in Mechanical Engineering. Mechanical Engineering Society; Athletic Association. Thesis: Design of Special Steel Underframing for Pullman Cars. "Dave" originated in the woods near Blue Island, Illinois. He attended Chicago Manual Training High School for a while, but hearing of the fame of Purdue, and being desirous of taking a course in "Hot Air" under "Jimmy," he emigrated to Lafayette. "Dave" is a wholesouled sort of a fellow; only swears when mad; and has but one failing—he will go to see the girls on Sunday night. He likes design, and is designing a car for his thesis that will make the Pullman product look like thirty cents.

Emily Kate Durkin blew in to Purdue from the Chicago suburbs, loving everything the Windy City has to offer—from the Chicago Blackhawks to the Magnificent Mile, the vibrant city culture, Broadway shows and opportunities, and even good 'ol Lake Michigan—those blustery winter days can't keep her down! She is not only a lover of all things Chicago, (minus the Chicago Cubs, of course), but a lover of all things history; no question it's her major—along with anthropology. She is known for her can-do positive attitude and a smile on her face. After graduation, she plans to attend graduate school, joining the Peace Corps to help others, and reciprocate her blessings, or working in a museum. In addition, she plans to travel the world, all the while never forgetting her Chicago roots.

JOE BURKE KNAPP, B. S. in Civil Engineering. Sigma Nu; Civil Engineering Society; Varsity Football Team (2) (3) (4); Manager (4); Class Baseball (1) (2); Athletic Association (1) (2) (3) (4), Vice-President (1); B. 0. L. M. Thesis: Investigation of the Coefficient of Expansion of Concrete. As a glorious sunset will often linger on a wintry sky, so "Joeie's" smile of wine-sap luster froze forever while he was carrying the Evansville *Morning Courier*. With a train of native contemporaries in 1900 he first sought a campus ticket from the famous "Sappho" Decker and spent his Freshman year introducing himself and acquiring friends, despite his bashful nature. After he had become an athletic star he let his light so shine before men that even the girls basked in it and he was forced to become a prize dog in society. In both these lines he has gained diplomas: in one, the injured knee of a Spartan; and in the other, the split lips of a Romeo. The world has knocked him about of late, but he now goes forth to knock about the world.

ALEXANDRIA "ALEX" NICKOLAS comes from a small college in Houston of the Lone Star State and brought with her the warm sunshine of Texas. She was known to always sit transfixed by a book or baking an assortment of sweets in her kitchen. While she is studious and meticulous about her schoolwork, she has a reputation of napping on the couch with her cat in her lap. She is an avid member of Purdue's Higher Ground Dance Company, a philanthropic group that raises money for disabled children to partake in dance therapy, and an initiate for Purdue's honor fraternity, Phi Sigma Pi. After graduation, she will go on to attain her doctorate in rhetoric and composition, and someday she plans to teach at a fine institution, much like Purdue.

Hugo Alex Berthold, B. S. in Electrical Engineering. Irving (r) (2) (3) (4), Treasurer (2), President (3), Marshal (-t-), Critic (4) ; Purdue Branch A. I. E. E. (4); Class Treasurer (3) (4); '04 Banquet Committee (2); Military Ball Committee · (4); Athletic Association (r) (2) (3) (4); Cadet Captain; *Exponent* Staff, Reporter (4); *Debris* Staff, Advertising Manager; Minuet Club; Senior Banquet Committee. Thesis: Distribution of Magnetism in Rotary Converters. Although Hugo has about evenly divided his time since his advent on this mundane sphere between this country and Germany, he is as thorough an American as any of us who have never been outside the limits of our own chicken yard.

He is a natural born promoter, and as soon as he gets interested in any project (he is connected with nearly every enterprise about the University) things have got to move. He is the champion leg-puller of the school—he can collect money off anybody and everybody—and comes mighty near being able to get blood out of the traditional turnip. He will succeed in any capacity where hustling is required. New York is his home.

LINDY E. SCHUBRING hails from the barren land of Gilbert, Arizona. When she is not huddled inside, longing for the warm desert weather, she is pursuing her love of dance and song. She studies hospitality and tourism management, and works as a campus tour guide. After graduation she hopes to work on a cruise ship, sailing the high seas and working as a food and beverage manager.

SUKICHI YOSHISAKA, B. S. in Electrical Engineering. Thesis: Design and Construction of Electromagnetic Absorption Dynamometer. Suckichi Yoshisaka, from Kobe, Japan, has been a most interested student of American slang. He took this up as a side line, starting his first year's tutelage under the efficient Professor Krause, making marked advancement and completing the course with an essay on "Dem Fool." He has here and in Ohio University, which he attended for some time, managed to obtain a surprising amount of electrical information, and is now formulating a wireless method of transmission by which he hopes to electrocute the entire Russian forces. He is at present experimenting on Karchoff as the nearest substitute for a Russian.

VIVIAN GU hails from West Lafayette, Indiana. Throughout childhood, she boasted an imaginative and free spirit that manifested itself in many hobbies over the years. From swimming, to woodworking, to mathematics, to fiction writing, she has many different passions. Nowadays, she floats amongst a sea of majors, guided only by a fervent desire to create, and strives eagerly toward the unknown future.

LYLA VIVIAN MARSHALL, B. S. in Science. Philalethean Literary Society (r) (2) (3), Secretary (r), Critic (r); *Debris* Staff, Artist (4). Thesis: French Impressionism. Lyla Marshall claims Lafayette as her home town, having received her education and spent most of her life here. Her younger days were spent at her father's country home, where she acquired her great love for nature and made her first efforts in an artistic line. Although taking the Science Course she has specialized in Art and expects to go on with the work. She will enter Art Institute next fall to study Illustrating.

CAROLYN GRIFFITH, B. S. in Management and Hospitality and Tourism Management. Black Tie Society, HTM Society, HTM Career Day Board Executive Assistant, Sigma Kappa Sorority, Delta Council. Hailing from Lafayette, Indiana, Carolyn spent her time at Purdue both fondly and condescendingly being referred to as a "townie." She has not served as an athletic light, but her greatest accomplishments included mastering the chocolate chip cookie and overachieving on group projects. Considered by her colleagues to be hard working and of well repute, Carolyn looks forward to a bright future in the hotel business realm. Upon graduation, she intends to relocate far from the Midwest region to satisfy her love of travel.

CECIL CLARE CRANE, B. S. in Science. Philalethean, Annuals (I) (4), Secretary (I) (2) (3), Censor (3), President (4); *Exponent* Staff (4) ; *Debris* Staff, Literary Editor (4). Thesis: The Idealism of George Sand. Cecil is one of our esteemed, even after frequent association with members of '03. She came to Lafayette from Bryan, Ohio, and went to the City High School here, where she fitted herself for a brilliant career at Purdue. As a wielder of the paste and shears she has furnished entertainment for many by her apt selections for the exchange pages of the *Exponent*. She has a lively spirit of humor, and likes to take a shy at her classmates in the form of roasts, an opportunity for which was afforded her by her position on the staff which is responsible for this book. When she finishes here she expects to indulge in school teaching for a time, unless—

CEDAR MARIE WOODWORTH hails from the woods of Cloverdale, Indiana. A modern-day Cinderella, she can often be found up to her elbows in sketching charcoal or sewing late into the witching hours in the apparel labs of Matthews Hall. It is rumored that before one particularly swift deadline, she slip stitched herself into a coma and awoke the next morning, surrounded not only by mannequins, but by a classroom full of students. When not loitering at a coffee shop or mumbling to herself in French, one may catch glimpses of the svelte amazon speeding around on her colorful bicycle. Self-described as a lover of "people, places, and things," she intends to carry her Victorian sense of humor, biting editorial critiques, and affinity for the color black into the fashion industry.

FREDERIC HENRY MILLER, B. S. in Electrical Engineering. Varsity Football (r) (z) (4); Insignia (4); Baseball Trainer (3); Minstrels (2) (3); Band (2) (3) (4); Insignia

Board (3); A. 0. D. D. Thesis: A Study of Single Phase Alternating Current Motors. "Happy" Miller, "The Prince" from Waynetown, is one of our number who has been able to partake of all the vices and virtues ordinarily allotted to the student without suffering in the least from either. From the time he first went after "Sunny Jim's" scalp-lock in Electrical Measurements Lab, until the smile was wiped from his face after the wreck, "Happy" was in one grand round of pleasure. No football team has been found with sufficient weight to crush out his everlasting grin, and the hardest flunk test failed to perturb his soul. The neverfading wreath of smiles which hangs on his front window indicates the state of mind within. May his shadow never grow less.

Paige S. Zimmerman journeyed to Purdue from the resilient town of Washington, Illinois, seeking to become an expert hotelier while at the same time drinking in the full experience of the Purdue "All-American" Marching Band. With her blue eyes set on a future making other people smile, her own infectious smile brightens the days of her fellow students while she continues on her educational path.

Harry Leon Hodges, B. S. in Civil Engineering. '04 Class Football Team (3); '02 Class Football Team (1) (2).

Thesis: Deflection of Bridges. Harry Leon Hodges, the "Kid," first smiled in West Lafayette in the year 1880. We pass hurriedly over the story of his early career, with its incidents of cut thumbs, stubbed toes and bumblebee stings common to all boyhood, merely stating that he grew up from a playful, irresponsible youngster to an irresponsible, playful man. At this juncture we find him entering Purdue with the class of 1902. Upon the arrival of the class of 1904, however, he at once perceived the opportunity of graduating with a famous class, and accordingly dropped out for two years, working (the Big Four R. R. Co.) in the meantime. If he survives the shock of getting his diploma, we will probably see him located next year in Gus's barber shop in the capacity of porter.

LILY ANNE ANDERSON was born on a farm in rural Carroll County, Indiana, and spent her pre-Purdue years wrangling ornery sheep and building hay forts. She would probably still be happily mucking about on the farm if not for an overwhelming desire to follow in her father's footsteps to become a doctor. She is extremely thankful for her loving family that has brought her to where she is today, and she is proud to call herself a Boilermaker along with her three older siblings. Though she now calls Purdue home, you will probably never see Lily on campus because she is exceptionally good at building textbook forts to hide beneath.